Professional Ethics and Librarians

Professional Ethics and Librarians

by Jonathan A. Lindsey
and Ann E. Prentice

ORYX PRESS
1985

The rare Arabian Oryx is believed to have inspired the myth of the unicorn. This desert antelope became virtually extinct in the early 1960s. At that time several groups of international conservationists arranged to have 9 animals sent to the Phoenix Zoo to be the nucleus of a captive breeding herd. Today the Oryx population is over 400 and herds have been returned to reserves in Israel, Jordan, and Oman.

Copyright © 1985 by
The Oryx Press
2214 North Central at Encanto
Phoenix, Arizona 85004-1483

Published simultaneously in Canada

Printed and Bound in the United States of America

Library of Congress Cataloging in Publication Data

Prentice, Ann E.
  Professional ethics and librarians.

  Bibliography: p.
  Includes index.
  1. Librarians—Professional ethics—United States.
I. Lindsey, Jonathan A., 1937–   . II. Title.
Z682.2.U5P75   1985   174'.9092'0973   83-43244
ISBN 0-89774-133-1

Table of Contents

Foreword

The average person is highly unlikely to have given a second—or even a first—thought to the question of the professional ethics of librarians. Think of the stereotype of a librarian: a bespectacled spinster with a pencil in her bun, dispensing novels to drowsy dowagers and shushing rowdy students. What could *that* image have to do with ethics at all? Further, what unethical conduct may have taken place on the part of librarians has seldom, if ever, made substantial news outside of the profession, and never has it risen to the *cause célèbre* level. Consequently, the nonlibrarian is as unfamiliar with library or information ethics as she or he is familiar with legal or medical ethics.

This lack of general knowledge regarding information ethics is attributable to the nature of our profession at this point in its development. In medicine and law, money changes hands between the professional and the client, and the services rendered can result in loss of money, of individual freedom, and, even, of life. Until recently money was not exchanged between librarian and user, and the consequences of service were always attributed to the source of information.

The circumstances that are changing the library profession began in the 1960s when computerized databases started charging for access to information, and vendors began to treat information as a commodity. In a technological age in which the volume of information generated increases exponentially, the librarian has been forced to pick and choose more carefully and, reluctantly, to charge users for services that go beyond the basic level. The more money changes hands, the more the client comes to rely on the information provided, the greater the consequences will be for the librarian who provides wrong or inaccurate information. As the librarian charges fees and makes judgments in the provision of service, the profession will quickly become equated with medicine and law, and information ethics will be commonplace. After a librarian is sued for providing misinformation, the subject of professional ethics will no longer be cause for a yawn.

Emphasizing this aspect of the library profession is not meant to downplay ethical conduct among librarians. It is generally accepted that the codes of conduct that pervade a free society are the basis for all ethical behavior and are followed in libraries as in other businesses and organizations. These codes are automatically included in any professional code. The distinguishing characteristic of person-to-person provision of customized, fee-based information service provides increasing numbers of occasions for abuse for personal gain. Ethical problems in this area are likely to arise more often than before.

It is appropriate then, almost 50 years after the American Library Association adopted its first statement on professional ethics, now twice revised, that a definitive history has been compiled. Having served on the Professional Ethics Committee for four years without benefit of significant background material, I am aware of the size of the task that the authors have undertaken. The transitional phase between a code that protected ourselves with "shoulds" to a code protecting our users with "musts" is critical to our evolution as responsible professionals. The authors were instrumental in shepherding the profession through that stage as were several of the librarians whose comments on the present code of ethics are included in this work.

As librarians are viewed more and more as *the* purveyors of information in this technological era, the persistent problem of a code of ethics without an enforcement mechanism will plague us. Regardless of one's view of the present code, the lack of penalties for breaching it keeps it in the realm of philosophy rather than reality. The authors examine this question through the exploration of methods of enforcement and the presentation of cases. They also chronicle for the first time the extensive discussions of this issue which took place in committee meetings and open hearings on the code.

This book brings us up-to-date on professional ethics and librarianship. More important, it gives us the basis from which to proceed into the information age as responsible and respected professionals accountable to ourselves as well as to our users.

Patrick M. O'Brien
Director of Libraries
Dallas Public Library
October 1984

Chapter 1
The Development of Ethics Codes

Members of society need to be assured that professionals will provide high-quality service free from any implications of personal gain. For this reason, ethical considerations, often formalized into codes, have been on society's agenda for well over 2,000 years. This continuous underlying concern for professional ethics gains attention from time to time, usually triggered by a major social event. In this century, such events occurred in the 1920s and again in the 1960s–70s. The relatively liberated era of the 1920s saw government scandal under Harding and engendered fears that the moral fabric of American society was breaking down. In the 1960s, a period of social upheaval, and in the 1970s, during and after the Watergate affair, concern was triggered for the ways in which we interact in our professional relationships. There was an implication that somehow we had become lax in our responsibilities to those we served and that we needed to re-examine our ethics. Librarianship, like many other professions, has taken part in this examination of its ethical bases; it developed a code which was approved by the Council of the American Library Association in 1981 and subsequently endorsed by most state associations.

To understand the process of developing an ethics code as it affects librarianship, one must place it in the larger context of professions, professional ethics, and the development of a professional ethic within the social environment. It is useful to see how other professions have approached the issue of developing their codes of ethics. Efforts by the American Library Association to develop a code can then be seen as part of larger trends rather than as something separate and unique.

Profession

A profession delivers esoteric services based on esoteric knowledge systematically formulated and applied to the needs of a client. Every

profession considers itself the proper body to set the terms in which
some aspect of society, life or nature is to be thought of, and to define
the general lines, or even the details of public policy concerning it.[1]

Certain basic features are common to all professions. The first require-
ment is an extensive period of training. In the past, this could be a
combination of formal education and an apprenticeship, but it has become
increasingly oriented toward formal education, usually in a university
setting. The law clerk who studied law under an established attorney as a
means of entering the profession has been replaced by the individual who
goes to law school to obtain a law degree. Although there is a physical and
intellectual component in all work activities, the intellectual component is
dominant in the professions. Professionals advise people how to do things
rather than doing the work themselves. For example, an architect—a
professional—designs living or work space for a client, while a builder—a
craftsperson—follows instructions and does the actual building.

Members of professions have autonomy in their work. They use their
judgment to determine the appropriate approach to their clients' problems.
Professionals can work independently and charge fees for specific services,
or they can be part of an organization such as a university, a clinic, or a
library and practice their professions within a larger context.

The abilities professionals acquire provide valuable services to society. The accountant, the lawyer, and the information professional are all
considered professionals because each provides a specific and unique
service important to the functioning of society. In providing these services,
the professional theoretically has no self-interest; interest in a particular
case or situation is the extent to which it sheds light on universal problems.
The professional is dedicated to the people and institutions served and takes
pride in the quality of professional service.

Professionals typically have their own associations which advance the
goals of the profession, promote the well-being of members, and develop
standards for the practice of the profession. The strength of the professional
organizations varies, and while some are very successful in promoting
member interests and policing members, others are not particularly strong
and provide support service rather than a more directive form of service.

Thus, professional behavior may be defined in terms of four essential
attributes:

> . . . a high degree of generalized and systematic knowledge; primary
> orientation to the community interest rather than to individual self-
> interest; a high degree of self-control of behavior through codes of
> ethics internalized in the process of work socialization and through
> voluntary associations organized and operated by the work specialists
> themselves; and a system of rewards (monetary and honorary) that is

primarily a set of symbols of work achievement and thus ends in themselves, not means to some end of individual self-interest.[2]

With the growing complexity of society in the twentieth century, there has been an increase in the number of new professions and a professionalization of occupations that were previously less complex. A software-design specialist is an example of the former; the librarian turned information specialist is an example of the latter. With this increasing number of professionals and the increasing complexity of what they do, problems of control over education for the profession, admission to the profession, and practice of the profession have become ever more complex.

Membership in professional associations varies a great deal. For some professions, association membership is by invitation only and carries with it considerable responsibility and prestige; others may open their membership to a broad range of individuals who may not be members of the profession but who may be interested in supporting the profession. The extent to which the association is successful in meeting its several expectations is to a large degree dependent upon the makeup of its membership.

The members of a professional association mutually guarantee not only their competence but also their honor and integrity. There are rules of conduct specific to a profession to which its members are expected to adhere. "This approach to problems of social conduct and social policy under the guidance of a professional tradition raises the ethical standard and widens the social outlook."[3] It is within the professional association that discussions of professional ethics typically take place and structures, both informal and formal, for guiding behavior toward clients and colleagues are devised. These structures or rules serve as controls and are typically more strict than those that are part of the legal system. This is due in part to necessity: "Only to the extent that society believes the profession is regulated by this collectivity orientation will it grant the profession much autonomy or freedom from lay supervision and control."[4]

The code of ethics of a professional association is a direct expression of its service orientation and its feelings of responsibility to its clientele. The code is specific to the profession, and only members of the profession are expected to adhere to it. It is enforced to varying degrees by the professional association; in fact, many formal codes have been devised and enforced by the professions to avoid coming under the regulations of other agencies. (Elements of codes may, however, be enforced by statute and administrative regulations.) "The code embodies the terms of an implicit contract between the professional and the society, by which the professional agrees to prevent its members from exploiting a potentially helpless layman and in return receives many privileges."[5]

Librarianship as a profession has shared in the overall concern for the development of a code of ethics. During the early to mid-twentieth century, librarianship became a full-fledged profession. It has since developed its body of theoretical knowledge, developed its educational and research components, and strengthened its professional associations. A strong service orientation has been characteristic of the profession from its beginning. In its development of a code of ethics, heavy responsibility has been placed on the shoulders of the educational component of the profession both in developing and disseminating a code.

The librarian-client relationship has limitations that do not exist to as great a degree in other professions. The librarian has little control over the client and must tailor service to fit within the knowledge limitations of the client rather than being able to impose his/her broader knowledge in a subject area. In serving clients, librarians are successful in the eyes of clients according to whether clients get what they think they want rather than necessarily what they need. The professional judgment of the librarian does not necessarily prevail, and the librarian may be perceived as harmless due to this lack of control over the client. But as librarianship has become a more technological profession, there is increasingly a perception that this "information specialist" may indeed have power to help or harm the client.

Ethics

Ethics is a system of values and rules that spell out what is right and what is good. It "is primarily concerned with the rightness, goodness and obligatory character or 'oughtness' of conduct. Ethics directly asks what kinds of acts are right or wrong, good or bad, or ought or ought not to be done, and what the terms involved mean."[6]

The earliest phase of ethics was tribal custom, later replaced by obedience to the decrees and laws of rules and councils. This in turn was replaced by a moral system wherein the responsibility for being ethical lay within the individual. Under such a system, the fitness of the act to the situation—doing the most good *under the circumstances*—determines its moral suitability. In 1930, W. D. Ross said that the fundamental concepts of ethics were right, good and morally good.[7] Right, Ross said, is an ambiguous term, as it can refer to the act that ought to be done because of a sense of duty or because it is morally right: A right act done out of a sense of duty may be morally wrong. "To assert that a certain level of conduct is at a given time absolutely right or obligatory is obviously to assert that more good or less evil will exist in the world, if it be adopted, than if anything else be done instead."[8]

According to Ross, right can and does mean "the cause of a good result." Rules and codes of conduct are ways of organizing responsibilities and agreeing on what is right, but it is dangerous to assume that, because we have agreed on what is right, we no longer need to think about it. Each issue must be examined to determine which response will produce the most good. Some duties rest on previous acts and are based solely on the wish to keep promises: We call this fidelity. Other duties are based on contractual agreements, rest on previous acts of others and one's wish to repay a favor, or rest on the possibility of making others happy through either beneficent behavior or not harming others.

Ethics was defined by the sociologist Emil Durkheim as "the rules which determine the duties that men owe to their fellows, solely as other men [and] form the highest point in ethics."[9] Durkheim believed that "a system of morals is always the affair of a group and can operate only if this group protects them by its authority . . . and that the greater the strength of the group structure, the more numerous are the moral rules appropriate to it and the greater the authority they have over their members."[10] No profession, then, can be without its own ethics, the means of regulating itself.

Ethical behavior has also been seen as an extension of legal doctrine. In those cases where a profession has not been able to police itself, laws have been passed to coerce people to meet appropriate standards. There has been much discussion as to the role that codes of ethics and laws play in governing the actions of those who work for the public good. The major difference is that codes are designed by professions for their own self-review, while laws are imposed from outside bodies. In addition, laws are more rigid than codes, and although subject to interpretation, they provide fewer situational opportunities for interpretation than codes of ethics. Both laws and ethics are an outgrowth of the culture and community of which they are a part. Although the applications may differ, the principles behind the codes of ethics and laws remain the same.

In situation ethics, people, not things, are at the center of concern. The basic issue is a pragmatic one: Does a decision help or hinder others? Those who support a situation ethic see cases from a world view rather than from a parochial view. There is a shift from language and logic to symbol and nondiscussive reasoning, a shift from rules or rationality to acceptance of unconscious and motivational dynamics, and a shift from a hierarchy of values to a positive spectrum.

History of Ethics Codes

Although there have been rules of conduct for professionals at least since the time of the ancient Greeks, the modern codes under which our society now operates date from the middle of the nineteenth century. The Code of Ethics of the American Medical Association was adopted in 1848 when the AMA was organized. It was a variation of a code published in England about 1803, written by the British physician Dr. Thomas Perceval. (Perceval's code was in the form of a letter to his son, who was entering the profession.) The code included elements of the laws of Hammurabi, which dealt with fees for service and with punishment when injury is done, and the oath of Hippocrates.

Between 1890 and 1924, more than 200 American business and professional groups adopted codes of ethics. The first code of ethics for the legal profession was adopted in 1908; additions were made in 1928 and 1933. The code spelled out what the courts could expect of attorneys in their attitude and deportment and set bans against conflict of interest, fee fixing, and undue influence of jurors. In the 1930s, the legal profession found that it had new problems that should be addressed through the code. These included a need for educational standards, the limiting of the number of new lawyers, and the need for strict disciplinary control and for a social conscience.

The teaching profession was slow to develop a code of ethics, in part because it used state-imposed standards as guidelines for conduct. During the 1920s, state education associations worked to draw up codes of ethics specific to the laws and educational concerns of their states, but these codes had their limitations. In 1926, commenting on these early educators' codes, Carl Tausch said that

> although [the codes] have manifestly arisen from a body of experi-
> ence, that experience has never been formulated into the objective and
> well-defined cases with which the lawyer and the engineer have
> worked. Indeed, the practice case in the teacher's ethical relation is
> unknown. Teachers codes contain many sentimental pleasantries that
> frequently amount merely to an innocuously idealistic creed. [They]
> aim to inspire ethical conduct into concrete cases or control it by
> practical sanctions.[11]

Tausch believed that teachers should sublimate their interests to the communities they served, be neat in appearance, and avoid material temptations. Although teachers were seen as necessary to the community, they were to be kept subservient to the community. The professional association and, to a degree, its code of ethics was to serve more as a control mechanism than as a support system. In 1929, the National Education Association, after four years of work, presented a code of ethics. It covered teachers' relationships to students, to the community, to the profession, and to colleagues.[12]

During the last 75 years, nearly every profession has considered and often adopted codes of ethics. The International City Management Association (ICMA) adopted its code of ethics in 1924 and has amended it five times since then, most recently in 1972 and 1976. The code addresses both beliefs (effective and democratic local government, dignity and worth of services, the service function of government) and responsibilities (implementing policies; maintaining communication; providing fair, high-quality service; seeking no favors).[13]

Interest in codes of ethics waned for some time during World War II and the 1950s, when concerns and priorities were directed toward international issues. In the last two decades, professional ethics has again become a topic of high interest.

In 1961, the American Marketing Association published a code outlining ethical practices for research users, practitioners, and field interviewers. Its purposes were to ensure accurate research results and to guarantee that market research would not be used as a vehicle for selling merchandise.[14] In 1966, responding to the renewed concern for ethics, the American Association of University Professors adopted a code of professional ethics. Its five items emphasize the need for intellectual honesty and for leading students in the free pursuit of learning. Responsibilities to the community of scholars, to the employing institution, and to the community are outlined. The code is directed to the individual and his/her behavior.

Within the scientific and engineering societies, considerable attention has been paid to ethical and legal issues. Engineering ethics codes date back to the nineteenth century and stress that the engineer's duty is to protect the public welfare; any activity that endangers the public welfare is unethical. The code of ethics for engineers developed from a codification of practice rather than from the more theoretical bases on which many other professional codes rest.

In the period from 1950 to 1970, the Committee on Scientific Freedom and Responsibility of the American Association for the Advancement of Science undertook a project to identify and describe the range of professional ethics activities in scientific societies and their codes and to suggest areas not covered that should receive attention. This project was motivated by several concerns, particularly the concern that "if the scientific societies are to continue to exercise their traditional professional autonomy, they will need to demonstrate that their ethical principles and rules of conduct serve society's interests as well as the interest of their own profession. . . ."[15]

There were additional concerns about both ethical and legal issues raised by the changing demands of society, such as the public expectations for accountability and consumers' demands to be informed, consulted, and protected. The changing roles of the professional, which had come to include consulting, advising, making policy, and delivering government service, all brought into question the extent to which existing codes addressed these questions.

Professions differ in the ethical issues that are most important to them and in the legal requirements that may affect them. Some professional societies have not only developed codes of ethics but have set up programs and activities to educate members about their profession's particular ethical questions and problems arising from relationships with colleagues, clients, institutions, and society.

Numerous surveys of professional ethics codes in science and engineering have been undertaken in the last 10 to 15 years. Peterson's 1969 review of associations of physical, natural, social, and applied scientists was done to determine if the associations had adopted ethical principles governing research. He found that many of the associations had established means of self-regulation, although not necessarily to the benefit of clients.[16] Trumbull's study in 1970 of 88 affiliated societies of the American Association for the Advancement of Science shows that 32 had codes, 2 subscribed to codes of other societies, 4 were considering codes, and 50 had none.[17] The Olan study in the mid-1960s of five social science associations showed that their efforts to develop codes were "generally unimpressive and politicized." Only one of the five had taken any effective steps to develop a code.[18] The Reynolds Survey (1973–1974) of 300 professional associations of social scientists resulted in 90 responses; only 24 associations had codes.[19] The codes tended to be routine and not useful in difficult situations; none had enforcement mechanisms.

The Blanspied/Shelanski Survey (1975) of 241 American Association for the Advancement of Science affiliates societies found that 45 of 80 respondents had codes.[20] Four additional surveys, The Frankel Survey (1975); Bureau of Social Science Research (1974); The Eaton Survey (1977–78); and the Wallace Survey (n.d.), were conducted in the 1970s; each indicated that codes of ethics and means of implementation were not a high priority for many associations.[21]

There was, however, increasing interest toward the end of the decade. Common themes in the surveys showed that a substantial number, but not a majority, had devised codes of ethics and that interest in adoption of codes had increased since the late 1960s. The 1979 project survey of its 241 member societies by the American Association for the Advancement of Science, for example, received a 74 percent response rate representing some 2 million members. Just over half of the respondents had a statement of ethical principles, usually in the form of a code. The lowest rate of adoption (18.2 percent) was among education and communication societies, with engineering (76.5 percent) having the highest rate of adoption.[22] An analysis of the codes submitted by participating societies included 191 distinct rules of conduct. Of these, only 6 rules are cited in 20 or more statements and 81 are mentioned only once. The ethical rules tended to be vague and poorly thought out, with the statements often ill defined or too abstract to be used in adjudication. The development of enforcement mechanisms tended to lag behind the development of the codes.

Ethics in the Public Sector

During the nineteenth century, the spoils system fostered unethical behavior, and government corruption was pervasive. The introduction of the merit system toward the end of the century returned a measure of integrity to government operations. Concern then shifted to the issues raised by the dehumanizing nature of large organizations and their effect on the individual. In recent years, political officials have come to define ethics as a problem of conflict of interest and public/private relationships of public officials.[23] In 1978, under the newly enacted Ethics in Government Act, an Office of Government Ethics was established under the Office of Personnel Management. The small agency, recognized ''as the sole independent legal implementing agency for conflict of interest and revolving door questions,''[24] serves as a consultant and gives advice on ethical issues prior to decision making. The act downplays the individual's sense of rightness in favor of legalistic responses; because of this, it has caused distress to those who see ethical behavior as a personal as well as a legal matter.

Since government service is a public trust, it is particularly important and particularly difficult to do what is ethical. The types of ethical problems confronting the individual in public service include implementation: Is a rule always right in every case? If the ethical stance of the organization is in conflict with those of the individual, which prevails? What happens to those who find the conflict between personal and organizational ethical standards intolerable?

These issues have received considerable attention in government since Watergate and ''attempts to probe the 'how to' of ethics training [has been seen to] require an understanding of the 'what.'''[25] Ethical conduct is more than staying out of trouble. Public employees are expected and entrusted to support the social/political values of responsiveness and fairness, the organizational values of loyalty and efficiency, the professional and peer values of expertise and cooperation, and the personal values of service and security.

Enforcement

As Alexis de Tocqueville once observed, Americans are always taking their moral temperature—an indication of the national wish to be moral and ethical. The implementation of codes of ethics is a general concern. Who should do it? Who has the power to do it, and if this is established, are the mechanisms available to enforce the codes? Responses range from "Let your conscience be your guide" to a demand for strict enforcement of specific ethics statements.

Following the Ethics in Government Act of 1978, the staff of the General Accounting Office did a study to determine a job's particular vulnerability to ethical problems. [26] Both the act and the study are results of public interest in clean government. The study indicated that tasks requiring discretion and those done in isolation were found to be most vulnerable. The overall attitude of the organization was the key to the level of ethical performance by the individual. Organizational factors that can affect an employee's ethical conduct include the absence of effective sanctions for dealing with improper actions, the lack of accountability expectations, and outmoded standards of ethical behavior. A laxness in the organization can relay the message to the individual that it is all right to be lax in personal activities and that rewards may be greater from unethical than from ethical behavior.

A survey conducted in 1979 by the American Association for the Advancement of Science found that very few of the responding societies allocated any funds for activities related to the enforcement of professional ethics. [27] Professional ethics responsibilities tended to be low priority for staff members. Some attention was paid to complaint handling but little data were gathered to determine what action was taken as a result of the complaints. Lacking a support structure to encourage and reward ethical behavior or penalties for nonethical behavior, professional associations have little clout in enforcement. The exceptions are those associations, such as the American Bar Association and the American Medical Association, that limit their membership to a specific group through examination or similar means and whose members' employment is dependent on that membership. The Library Association in the United Kingdom also meets these criteria, and the enforcement of its code of ethics is strict.

A more common model is that of the International City Managers Association. Its executive board is responsible for wide dissemination of the code, for providing positive guidance to its membership through interpreting the code, and for offering advisory opinions. The code has been used in support of members under attack in localities and to discipline members. The rules assure due process; although this is slow, it is fair. Members are concerned that as the professional association grows it may ''outgrow its ability to enforce the code in the fair, personal way possible in a smaller organization.''[28]

Enforcement may be difficult, not only because of the relative weakness of many professional associations but also because of external influences. Politicians and pressure groups may have an interest in a particular outcome in an ethical issue and may exert pressure on an association to meet its objectives, perhaps to the detriment of the association or to ethical principles. There is an attitude among many professionals that codes of ethics are too broadly written and couched in platitudes, that they may even be self-serving, and that they are certainly unenforceable. Their response is to ignore the code or not to take it seriously. The professional has a code of behavior that gives direction to his/her entire life, and part of this life is the professional component. Many professionals see no need for a specific code of behavior to cover just one aspect of their lives. As is true with many laws and regulations, it is not the law-abiding citizen who needs them, but those who do not have the best interest of society in mind. Ethics is intended to provide limits to behavior, thus keeping the less ethical population within the bounds of ethical behavior. Part of learning ethical behavior is the conditioned response of reward and punishment. The concept of self-respect keeps the honest individual from unethical behavior.

The most realistic means of ethics enforcement in our diverse society would include the presence of a written and agreed-upon code of ethics, education of the members of the profession to the ethical constraints on professional conduct, and the application of peer pressure to enforce the code. Codes can help justify, but they can not compel action.

> Codes of ethics can, within limits, help to sensitize members to ethical constraints on professional conduct [as] ethics codes are valuable to educate (in substance, in development, and in training new professionals) and to bolster the person who tends to be ethical in situations fraught with counter-pressures. Ethics codes are meaningless without support (via professional societies and legislation).[29]

Further, codes are useful in defining professional responsibility. Self-regulation is necessary to a profession, and the review of a code of conduct serves to ensure that professional privileges and obligations are continuously reviewed. Finally, codes can provide a model of ethical behavior that members of a profession can follow.

As a summary of their study of professional ethics, the American Association for the Advancement of Science group prepared the following series of recommendations which can serve as a guide for any profession developing and implementing a code of ethics.*

1. The scientific and technical societies should develop programs and activities to sensitize both their members and the public to the values affecting the development and use of professional knowledge. The societies should recognize that such values will be considered in a casual and ad hoc manner in the absence of institutional activities designed to bring them to member attention. The societies' emphasis on such programs should at the very least be consistent with the size and scope of their organizational activities as a whole.

   The activities of the societies should supplement and support the concept of the individual professional acting as an independent moral agent, and, where appropriate, they also should include rules and guidelines to help resolve conflicts in cases where the society's members have reached a consensus on the proper course of professional conduct.

2. The societies should strive to identify the basic ethical principles which represent the shared aspirations of their professions. These principles should clarify the ethical "goods" of the profession and the reasons why such "goods" are important to professional work. The principles should be clarified through discussions at society meetings and interpretive articles and should be distributed to all applicants for society membership.

3. The societies should recognize that ethical principles are guidelines, not rules, which cannot be imposed or broken. When conflicts arise among principles, however, societies should develop rules of conduct both to guide member's choices and to establish a public standard of behavior against which allegations of abuse or unprofessional conduct might be judged.

   Ethical rules can acknowledge selected ethical principles, but the societies should distinguish between the two in their formal statements. Statements of principles can be used as a statement of the ethical ideals of the profession in an educational sense. Statements of rules for professional behavior, on the other hand, should serve a regulatory function. Societies which adopt "educational codes" will sensitize their members and the public to values which are of importance to their profession. But such codes cannot serve as the basis for adjudicating complaints of "unprofessional behavior." On the other hand, rules which specify standards of member conduct and which offer a basis for adjudication and enforcement may not recognize broader values involved in professional work.

   Thus, each approach has unique advantages and disadvantages. Educational codes may be more appropriate for newly formed disci-

---

plines or small, homogeneous societies. Societies whose members work in many employment settings may require standards which specify more clearly the norms governing the behavior of their members in order to establish common approaches within the profession to resolve ethical conflicts in the application of professional knowledge.

4. Societies should prepare rules of professional conduct which can be understood easily both by the members and those affected by the member's professional work. Members should have an opportunity to acknowledge that they are familiar with the ethical rules of their profession and that they expect to follow them as a condition of their membership in the society. Efforts should be made to educate the general public about the societies' rules, and employers should also be informed about the existence of such rules by the societies. Any conflicts between the societies' rules and employers' policies should be addressed in a way that re-affirms the public service tradition of the professions.

5. Rules of professional conduct should be accompanied by procedures for adjudicating complaints and providing society sanction or support actions (if necessary). Every society that adopts such rules should establish a recognized procedure by which complaints of unprofessional conduct or requests for assistance can be brought to the attention of authorized representatives of the society.

6. Societies should recognize that principles or rules which place a paramount concern on protecting the health and safety of the public may place their members in conflict with their employers. Societies that received member requests for assistance (as a result of conflicts arising from member adherence to society rules) should try to provide support services to their members, including counseling and mediation activities, and, if necessary, financial or legal aid.

7. Professional societies should ensure that serious allegations of unprofessional conduct, whether raised by persons within or outside the profession, are reviewed in a manner that provides a fair and thorough review for all parties. In particular, the societies should develop policies regarding access to and disclosure of information collected in the course of adjudication and enforcement activities.

Such reviews may be time-consuming and costly, and if a large number of complaints are received, societies may need financial support to implement fair review and resolution of serious disputes. Experimental models for review should be evaluated and funded by the societies and others who wish to facilitate the resolution of such disputes in a fair and objective manner.

8. Professional societies should conduct periodic reviews of values important to their members' work. Changes in these values—and the emphasis placed upon them—will occur and should be expected given the changing social context for developing and applying scientific and technical knowledge. If conducted every four or five years, these reviews should provide an opportunity for the societies to identify new trends and areas of potential conflict requiring further attention.

Professional journals and newsletters should be encouraged to poll their readers from time to time to identify ethical concerns and report on individual cases raising significant issues for the profession.

9. The societies periodically should publish and distribute a report on the "State of Professional Ethics" in their professions. The report should include information on the society's ethics activities, identify members and staff working in this area, review the number of types of complaints or requests for support received by the society, and report the resolution of these cases. The report also should refer to pertinent society publications and summarize future activities.

10. The societies should coordinate their professional ethics activities to call attention to concerns that cut across disciplinary lines. To facilitate such coordination, primary responsibility for addressing professional ethics concerns should be assigned to a senior staff and/or a concerned member in each society.

11. Representatives of the public and private groups affected by the professional work of scientists and engineers should have an opportunity to express their concerns to the societies' members. The societies should establish visible and accessible channels for such exchange of views, including open forums at the societies' annual meetings, guest editorials in the societies' journals, and other approaches. Societies whose members are licensed for public service should consider appointing public representatives to review boards or licensing panels.

12. Professional societies should recognize that they are one of several groups—including employers and non-governmental and governmental organizations—which develop rules and guidelines affecting the professional work of scientists and engineers. This mix of institutional factors produces a formal and informal regulatory system which directly affects the values that shape the development and application of scientific and technical knowledge. Ethical concerns and conflicts often highlight values that may not be shared universally—or shared with equal emphasis—by these various institutions.

    The societies should be alert and responsive to such concerns, providing opportunities to review various perspectives on controversial ethical issues for their members in a timely fashion.

13. The societies should actively seek to ensure that those organizations which employ their members recognize the importance of ethical concerns associated with the development and application of science and technology. The societies should urge employers to provide formal channels to resolve differences of opinion precipitated by moral values in conflict between their professional and management staffs. The existence of such dissent procedures should be considered an essential part of a professional working environment in large organizations.

14. The range of activities pursued by the societies is affected by internal and external forces as well as by contemporary and historical trends. Yet knowledge of the influence wielded by these factors is seriously undernourished. Case studies of individual societies over time as well as comparative studies involving two or more societies should improve our understanding of the interaction between the societies and their external environment and of the impact that such interaction has on the societies' actions.

15. It is fair to say that we do not have well-defined benchmarks for evaluating the performance of the scientific and engineering societies on matters of professional ethics. Nor are there widely accepted and experienced institutional mechanisms guaranteed to improve the quality of the societies' performance. The societies and those outside who are concerned with their performance should conduct studies designed to identify useful criteria and to apply these criteria to measure and evaluate the full range of ethics activities implemented by the societies. This will not only advance the state of theoretical and empirical analysis of the professions and their ethics activities, but it will also generate alternative strategies which the societies could employ effectively to fulfill their institutional responsibilities related to professional ethics.

Future Issues

Ethics has its roots in our religious and legal traditions. It is also influenced by social environment. Our highly technological society demands a high order of compliance, a low level of sabotage, an adequate supply of qualified people, and a supportive surrounding society. If it is to work at all, it needs a high level of social interaction. In this society, "ethics may not be the primary determinant of the future but could be marginally influential."[30]

All professions are being asked to justify their services and to indicate what they are contributing to society. A profession must establish that its reason for existence is more than just the self-interest of its members. Accountability of government agencies and services has been an expectation of the electorate for several years. That expectation of accountability is now affecting the professions, and we must have valid responses to justify our profession and its contributions.

A second factor which is affecting the professions—and particularly, librarians—and their codes of conduct is the broadening opportunities resulting from the massive technological innovation of the recent past. Technological change will continue to be rapid in the next decade, creating even more possibilities and problems for professionals.

The amount of information available through access to computerized databases and the ability to manipulate that data in many ways presents a potential for misuse of data on a larger scale than ever before. The ethical questions regarding what is authorized and what is unauthorized use of data are becoming an issue of concern in both the public and the private sector. Should an employee, for example, use the company computer for personal use? IBM says no, that all company systems are for business use only; other companies such as General Electric and Equitable Life do not object to and may even encourage employee use of company computers.[31] Additional concerns arise because of the accessibility of information via computer including product information, research information, and personnel information. "Some corporate executives contend that it is unethical for an employee to browse through a desk drawer. But employees do not always feel that way. They equate computer files to electronic bulletin boards, open to such browsing."[32]

Guidelines for what is private information and what is not vary, and given the attitudes toward information available through computer manipulation, misuse can be a problem. The issue of copying software is both a legal and ethical question. Many workers store data in their personal computers to work on at leisure or they may set up individual data banks which may include confidential personal information. The ability of supervisors to monitor these data banks may violate the worker's privacy in another way as supervisors can also monitor work flow by computer and thus control the individual to an extent greater than previously possible. Some companies are developing policies to deal with the issues of electronic access while others see no difference between a data bank and a filing cabinet.

A study of computer use and abuse was conducted recently under an NSF grant and led to a project on computer-specific ethical issues.[33] The following ethical issues for which there are no rules or guidelines were identified.

- Repositories and processors of information. Unauthorized use of otherwise unused computer services of information stored in computers raises questions of appropriateness or fairness.
- Producers of new forms and types of assets. Computer programs are entirely new types of assets, possibly not subject to the same concepts of ownership as other assets.
- Instruments of acts. To what degree must computer services and users of computers, data, and software be responsible for the integrity and appropriateness of computer output?
- Symbols of intimidation and deception. The images of computers as thinking machines, absolute truth producers, infallible, subject to blame, replacements for human errors, and anthropomorphic in nature should be carefully considered.[34]

It was recognized by the American Federation of Information Processing Societies (AFIPS) that there was a need for formalized ethical standards to respond to these issues, and in 1970 it sponsored a meeting on professionalism in the computer field. Some AFIPS constituent groups had developed codes of ethics but had not tested their enforcement. The codes had not been applied and therefore there was no interpretation. Legal aspects of computer use are gradually being dealt with, but ethical questions still require attention. Under an NSF grant, the American Federation of Information Processing Societies developed an approach to the discussion of ethical issues through a scenario approach. Experts were sent a scenario and asked to respond to the ethical issues involved. From their responses, ways of dealing with situations were identified. The project summary included a list of ethical issues and the responses given, including the obligations of users of computer services.[35] The privacy issue was of particular importance, and professionals were urged to use information only in socially acceptable ways. Several information and computing associations, including the American Society for Information Science, have developed codes of ethics to address these ethical issues. As with earlier codes, they tend to be general, high-minded, and probably unenforceable.

As our society continues to change in its expectations of science and technology, and in its expectations of its professionals, new ethical issues will continue to emerge.

References

1. Kenneth Lynn and the Editors of *Daedalus, The Professions in America* (Boston: Houghton Mifflin, 1965), p. 3.
2. Bernard Barber, "Some Problems in the Sociology of the Professions," in *The Professions in America*, p. 18.
3. Howard M. Vollmer and Donald L. Mills, eds., *Professionalization* (Englewood Cliffs, NJ: Prentice-Hall, 1966), p. xi.
4. Vollmer and Mills, p. 37.
5. Vollmer and Mills, p. 41.
6. Thomas E. Hill, *Ethics in Theory and Practice* (New York: Thomas Y. Crowell Co., 1956), p. 2.
7. W. D. Ross, *The Right and the Good* (Oxford: Clarendon Press, 1930).
8. Ross, p. 9.
9. Emil Durkheim, *Professional Ethics and Civil Morals* (Glencoe, IL: The Free Press, 1958), p. 3.
10. Durkheim, p. 7.
11. Carl F. Tausch, *Professional and Business Ethics* (New York: Henry Hold and Co., 1926), p. 141.
12. Ibid.
13. William Besuden, "The Profession's Heritage: The ICMA Code of Ethics," *Public Management* (March 1981): 2.
14. Dick Warren Twedt, "Why a Marketing Research Code of Ethics?" *Journal of Marketing* 27 (October 1963): 48–50.
15. R. Calk, M. S. Frankel, and S. B. Chafer. "Professional Ethics Activities in the Scientific and Engineering Societies" (AAAS project, 1980), p. 2.
16. Calk, Frankel, and Chafer, p. 10.

17. Ibid.
18. Calk, Frankel, and Chafer, p. 11.
19. Ibid.
20. Calk, Frankel, and Chafer, p. 12.
21. Calk, Frankel, and Chafer, pp. 13–14.
22. Calk, Frankel, and Chafer, p. 21.
23. James S. Bowman, ''Special Symposium Issue: Ethics in Government,'' *Public Personnel Management* 10 (1) (1981): 6.
24. Bowman, p. 6.
25. Bowman, p. 41.
26. U.S. General Accounting Office, *Framework for Assessing Job Vulnerability to Ethical Problems* (Washington, DC: GAO, 1981).
27. Calk, Frankel, and Chafer, p. 52.
28. International City Managers Association, ''City Management Code of Ethics,'' *Public Management* (March 1981): 4–5.
29. Calk, Frankel, and Chafer, p. 61.
30. Rufus E. Miles, Jr., *Awakening from the American Dream: The Social and Political Limits to Growth* (New York: Universe Books, 1976), p. 222.
31. ''Computer Ethics: New Questions Arise over Misuse in American Business,'' *New York Times,* (December 25, 1983), p. 1.
32. ''Computer Ethics,'' p. 13.
33. Donn B. Parker, *Ethical Conflicts in Computer Science and Technology* (Arlington, VA: AFIPS Press, n.d.).
34. Parker, p. 2.
35. Parker, p. 14.

Chapter 2
American Library Codes of Ethics: A Documentary Approach

Codes of ethics, or even official statements on the part of library associations, have not been burning professional issues during the several centuries of American librarianship. The question appears to have been irrelevant prior to 1900, and some would say that it has been of little relevance since. After all, members of the American Library Association (ALA) have considered adopting official statements on ethics only four times in the association's history: in 1929, 1938, 1975, and 1981. (The latter two should probably be seen as a single, evolving effort.) Both the California Library Association and the Ohio Library Association adopted statements on professional ethics in 1975; they are the only state associations to have done so. At its June 1984 annual meeting, the ALA Council Committee on Professional Ethics reported that 44 state or regional associations and 5 divisions of ALA have endorsed the 1981 Statement of Professional Ethics with a Code of Ethics for librarians. One state association, Wyoming, specifically voted not to endorse the 1981 statement.

In 1922, when members of the American Academy of Political and Social Science entertained the question of professional ethics, they did so under the rubric of "The Ethics of the Professions and Business." Included in the Academy's *Annals* of that year was a series of essays from a variety of professional groups; among those asked to contribute were librarians. Charles Knowles Bolton, secretary and librarian of Boston Athenaeum, presented the ethical concerns faced by American librarians.[1] Through Bolton's 1922 summary, noted in *Library Journal*,[2] an indication was presented of his concern and the concerns of his fellow Bostonians with ethical questions for librarians.

Bolton identified Mary W. Plummer, director of the Pratt Institute Library School in Brooklyn, New York, as having raised the question and initiated a test for a code of ethics for librarians in a paper that she read at the 1903 Illinois Library Association. At the time, Plummer chaired an ALA committee to investigate library education and "report on the various library schools and training classes."[3] Her initial concern in setting forth her views was "the claims of librarianship to be called a profession,"[4] a concern that has not abated. Plummer set out four essentials for the preparation of librarians: bibliographic knowledge, knowledge of technique, knowledge of administration, and personal preparation. The fourth essential, personal preparation, was the subject of a leaflet: below are two versions of it. The first is from the 1903 *Public Libraries* record of her address, the second from the *Annals*, in which Bolton claimed as a source Plummer's "own revised copy."[5] The texts are essentially the same, except for paragraph structure and the wording of the final paragraph.

1903	1922

There is a fourth essential for librarianship, and a last, for in all this I am taking the general educational qualification for granted. This fourth essential is the personal preparation. If we compare the professions with the trades we at once realize there is a difference in their personnel. Doctors, lawyers and ministers, college professors, officers of the army and navy, have a certain code which presupposes that they are gentlemen, and wish to remain so. A breach of this etiquette strikes at the foundations of their order.

Librarians and educators in general have their code still to make. Craftsmen and tradesmen may have a code, but if so, its exigencies are less. The fact that these codes are for the most part unwritten makes them no less binding; they are like debts of honor which, although unrecorded, must be paid first of all debts. If we were making a code for librarian-

Doctors, lawyers and ministers, college professors, officers of the army and navy, have a certain code which presupposes that they are gentlemen and wish to remain such. A breach of this etiquette strikes at the foundations of their order.

Librarians and educators in general have their code still to make. The fact that these codes are for the most part unwritten makes them no less binding; they are like debts of honor, which, although unrecorded, must be paid first of all debts. If we were making a code for librarianship, what would it have to be to help that calling to rank among the profes-

ship, what would it have to be to help that calling to rank among the professions? Surely the following would be some of its requirements:

We must have dignity, and if we have to advertise, we must be careful how we do it.

We must have humility; all boasting of ourselves or of our work is out of place.

We must realize our individual limitations and be willing to learn before we try to teach.

We must consider our work one of humanity, and must be ready, like doctors, to attend to pressing cases, in season and out of season. Too rigid holding to hours in one's work savors of the trades-union.

We must have esprit de corps, and librarianship must be even more than now a sort of free-masonry.

We must believe in our work, quietly, not ostentatiously.

We must suppress our natural tendencies where they conflict with the best interests of the profession, and if necessary, be willing to give up the work for the good of the work. This is a hard saying, and it may sound Irish to give it as an instance of preparation for librarianship, but you will see what I mean. Suppose that it comes to my ears that I am said to be too loud, too boisterous, too flippant and familiar, to be in charge of a library, or even on its staff. The thing to do is not to get angry, but to keep a sharp lookout that this criticism shall no longer have the least foundation. And suppose I hear that my methods are antiquated, that I prefer ruts and my own comfort to the service of the public; it is plainly my duty not to resent this without self-examination, and if I

sions? Surely the following would be some of its requirements:

We must have dignity, and if we have to advertise, we must be careful how we do it.

We must have humility. All boasting of ourselves or of our work is out of place.

We must realize our individual limitations and be willing to learn before we try to teach.

We must consider our work one of humanity, and must be ready, like doctors, to attend to pressing cases, in season and out of season. Too rigid holding to one's hours savors of the trades-union.

We must have esprit de corps, and librarianship must be, even more than now, a sort of free-masonry.

We must believe in our work, quietly, not ostentatiously.

We must suppress our natural tendencies, where they conflict with the best interests of the profession, and, if necessary, be willing to give up the work for the good of the work.

It comes to my ears that I am said to be too loud, too boisterous, too flippant and familiar to be in charge of a library, or even on its staff. The thing to do is not to get angry, but to keep a sharp lookout that this criticism shall no longer have the least foundation.

I hear that my methods are antiquated, that I prefer ruts and my own comfort to the service of the public. It is plainly my duty not to resent this without self-examination, and if I find it true, either to infuse more energy and self-denial into my character or to yield my place to some one who can fill it worthily.

find it true, either to infuse more energy and self-denial into my character, or to yield my place to someone who can fill it worthily.

In short, every one of us should say to himself or herself, Am I personally, a credit to librarianship, and if not, what is wrong with me? Am I helping to make librarianship a profession, or am I hindering?[6]

We should say to ourselves, Am I, personally, a credit to librarianship, and if not, what is wrong with me? Am I helping to make librarianship a profession, or am I hindering?*

Bolton noted essays by two other persons who followed Plummer. One was by Genevieve M. Walton, the other by Linda M. Duvall. Walton's essay, according to Bolton, was general in its statements.[7] Walton's essay, given in 1904 as an address to the Michigan Library Association, raised three areas of concern which have continued to be reflected in each statement of ethics by librarians in America in the twentieth century: (1) the relation of librarian to fellow librarian; (2) the relation of librarian to official superior under whom he serves . . . the relation of the librarian to his co-workers. . . ; (3) the relation of the librarian to the public. . . .[8] Walton lamented the lack of interest in ethics reflected in her fruitless search through the index of *Library Journal*, Poole's *Index,* and other standard reference sources of the day.

Bolton further acknowledged the interest of a group of Boston librarians whose occasional dinner meetings between 1908 and 1909 had led to the development of a proposal for a code of library ethics. In 1909, Bolton's version of the implied consensus of an unnamed group of Boston librarians was published in *Public Libraries.*

Taking up first the librarian's relation to his trustees we have:

I.   Responsibility
     In the organization of a library by the trustees much of their authority is usually delegated to the librarian. He should not chafe if the trustees as a body feel called upon from time to time to exercise the authority vested in them as guardians of the public interest.

II. Loyalty
     When a librarian cannot in his dealings with the public be entirely loyal to a policy which is clearly upheld by his trustees

---

*Reprinted from "The Ethics of Librarianship: A Proposal for a Revised Code" by Charles Knowles Bolton in Volume CI of *The Annals* of The American Academy of Political and Social Science. Copyright, 1922, by The American Academy of Political and Social Science. All rights reserved.

he should explain his position to the board, and in an extreme case offer to resign.

III.   Sincerity
To delay bringing a plan before the trustees until it is certain to obtain adequate presentation and a fair hearing may be considered only common wisdom; but to abstain from urging a project until a known opponent happens to be absent is unprofessional.

Turning now to the second of our subjects, the librarian's attitude toward those with whom he labors from day to day, we have these canons:

IV.   Duty to the staff
A librarian is bound, as opportunity offers, to advance those that are capable to more responsible positions in his own library or elsewhere. He must also spend the money of his institution with due prudence, and get a full return for it in service. Although efficiency of the staff is temporarily reduced by frequent transfer of assistants to new positions or to other libraries, in the end, a library whose workers are seen to obtain rapid and solid advancement profits by its reputation in this respect.

V.   The staff's duty to the librarian
A librarian has a right to entire loyalty from his staff, although he may be called upon at times to face frank comment from them. Such criticism should never go beyond the library doors; nor should the staff carry complaints over the librarian's head to the trustees, except in extreme cases.

VI.   The staff's duty to the library
An assistant should not allow personal antagonisms within the library to injure efficiency; nor should the staff use library hours for social intercourse. Enforced leisure during library hours should be used for self improvement as the best return for compensation received.

A librarian owes much to other librarians and to the professional associations, which are created for mutual benefit. We are not free lances engaged in warfare with our fellow workers. In these relations we have:

VII.   Expert advice
A librarian may not act as an expert adviser to the trustees of another library, even when solicited, without the request, or at least without the full knowledge, of the librarian concerned, and not then unless he is persuaded that serious and probably irremediable deliquencies exist. The analogy is to be found in the physician, who may not advise a patient unless the attending physician requests it, or until the attending physician has been dismissed.

VIII. Private advice
A librarian should feel free to claim counsel from others in the same calling, and should be willing to give such counsel when requested, without publicity or expense.

IX. Rivalry
Statistics should not be used to show superiority of a library over neighboring libraries, by making a comparison in figures which a librarian would think too discourteous to put into words. If there is to be printed criticism it should always bear clearly the librarian-author's name.

X. Engaging an assistant
A librarian may not negotiate for the services of an assistant in another library until he has made his intention known to the assistant's superior officer.

XI. Predecessors
A librarian who makes a habit of commenting unfavorably on the work of his predecessors in office invites criticism of his good taste.

Still another canon may be added to our list:

XII. A librarian's province
The librarian is endeavoring to be a force in the community, and contact with people even more than with books engenders force. We must not confuse the duties of librarian and assistant; the one is always associated with *people*, although in a small library he (or she) may do all the work; the assistant may or may not be called upon to meet the public, but generally has specific duties to which specific hours must be given.

XIII. Bearing in public
A librarian as a person of influence, and seeking the respect of all his fellow citizens, cannot carelessly choose his company nor indulge in habits and taste that offend the social or moral sense. These self-limitations are in the nature of hostages which he gives for the general good. He must not limit his advisors to one circle, for he needs a wide horizon, ready sympathies, and the good will of all classes.

XIV. Use of his name
A librarian should be chary of lending his name to a public controversy to add weight to the contention of a local faction, or to commercial enterprises, even those that have an educational or philanthropic motive. Having a financial interest in any material device, invention or book proposed for purchase in his library, the librarian should inform his trustees of this interest.

Beyond this there is a limitless field for our canons of ethics to cover. We cannot hope to mention all the ways in which librarians may be stimulated to high ideals. In his personal relation to books we may say:

XV. Specializing
The librarian should not permit specialized book-collecting or book-reading to narrow his field of interest, nor to bias his judgment in purchasing books. The number of points of contact with knowledge and with his public determines to some extent the librarian's usefulness.

In his relation to agents:

XVI. Shrewdness
Abandoning a reliable agent to obtain slightly better terms is usually of but temporary advantage, deprives the librarian of a trusted adviser and discourages a high standard in business. Nor should he jeopardize his independence by accepting special favors from business firms. The repudiation of orders and the return of books worn by reading injure the librarian's reputation for honorable dealing.

And, finally:

XVII. Professional spirit
A high professional spirit calls for sound training, clear ethical standards, and sustained enthusiasm for the fellowship of librarians.[9]

Bolton reported that, after three years' discussion and revision, eight sections were added to the 1909 document. The May 1912 *Public Libraries* carried only a note that Bolton was reprinting his code.[10] Bolton also indicated that in 1913 and 1914 his statement was discussed in ALA Executive Committee. The 1914 Midwinter Council was apparently at one point a forum for Josephine A. Rathbone to raise a question of ethics under a question of ''professional etiquette.'' Her illustrations, recorded in detail, dealt with the process by which a library assistant might be recruited by a librarian in another library. Rathbone submitted her definition of etiquette: ''crystallization of public opinion as to fitting and courteous conduct under certain well recognized circumstances.''[11] The consensus of the Council on January 2, 1914, was that it was inconceivable that any librarian would place obstacles in the way of a colleague.

One certainly does not infer lively debate when *Library Literature* reveals only six articles on a subject between 1909 and 1938, although ALA minutes reveal more concern and action. Some dialog must have been generated by Bolton, however, because in 1921 a paper and resultant article appeared, ''Professional Ethics for Librarians from the Point of View of the Library Assistant.''[12] Lavinia B. Kirkman Penley, a book order assistant in the Pomona Public Library, read the paper at the California Library Association meeting in Riverside, California, in 1921. She did not present a code of ethics, but she addressed questions that had been raised previously by Bolton. Penley, however, provided two important perspectives. The first was a definition of ethics: "Man's duty in respect to himself and the rights of others."[13] The second was a statement of the concerns of librarians and the responses of her sample of 30. These concerns centered on the following: personal characteristics, staff relationships, trustee relationships, and professional behavior. She provided a two-sentence summary to capture the essence of her presentation: "The assistant should always give the best service possible, should make every effort to fit himself for better work, should be fair to the chief and the library in the matter of giving notice. The librarian and trustees should give encouragement, inspiration, and compensation both as to salary and to recognition."[14]

In 1922, Bolton presented in the *Annals* his version of a 30-section code, which took into consideration the discussions of the ALA Executive Committee during 1913–1914, some 25 unnamed "leading librarians," and 14 other librarians who received named acknowledgment for their contributions to the 1922 statement. Bolton's aspiration for these "canons of ethics" was high because, he said, they stood "in the position of counselor . . . combining worldly wisdom and unworldly ideals."[15] In this code, articles 1–6 deal with trustees, 7–21 with staff relationships, and 22–30 with what would now be called professional matters. Bolton annotated each of the 30 articles in the 1922 version. For a full perspective it is helpful to see his commentary.

ARTICLE*	COMMENTARY*
I. Responsibility In the organization of a library by the trustees, much of their authority is usually delegated to the librarian. He should not chafe if the trustees as a body feel called upon from time to time to exercise the authority vested in them as guardians of the public interest.	In a large library a tactful and efficient librarian will accumulate power by that factor in human nature which delegates responsibility as rapidly as an executive officer proves his fitness to exercise authority. This is a menace to the librarian's character unless he returns again and again to the trustees as the

*Reprinted from "The Ethics of Librarianship: A Proposal for a Revised Code" by Charles Knowles Bolton in volume CI of *The Annals* of The American Academy of Political and Social Science. Copyright, 1922, by The American Academy of Political and Social Science. All rights reserved.

II. Authority

Under proper conditions the librarian to whom the entire board delegates authority should be able to exercise more power than any single trustee; and since the policy of looking to the librarian for results requires that a considerable measure of authority be delegated to him, habitual distrust of his judgment or disregard of his recommendations may well lead him to seek opportunity for usefulness elsewhere.

III. Alliances

A librarian should not ally himself with one trustee to the exclusion of other members of the board from his confidence.

IV. Loyalty

When a librarian cannot, in his dealings with the public, be entirely loyal to a policy which is clearly upheld by his trustees, he should indicate to the public, as far as possible, the reasons for this policy without expressing his own opinion; he should also explain his position to the board, and in an extreme case offer to resign.

source of his authority. He must show readiness to assume responsibility without becoming a law unto himself.

In a small library where the trustees comprise the few men and women of literary influence in the town the librarian receives a meagre salary, works for short periods, and is often of necessity a clerk or desk attendant in fact although librarian in name. The delegation of administrative authority to a single trustee is here practical. In the case of a large library this would be destructive of all librarianship. The trustees do a greater service by replacing an incompetent librarian by a new one than by assuming themselves the burden of his work.

If a librarian is to confide in one trustee more than in another this should be the chairman of his board or of a committee, a difficult and embarrassing course where the chairman appears to be indifferent and another trustee earnest and peculiarly congenial. But to avoid the pitfall of social, racial or religious cliques he is better off in moderate isolation than as the intimate of a faction. Although the librarian thinks that he knows the type of trustee best suited to the need of his town he is on dangerous ground if he attempts to influence the selection of a trustee.

Stress should be placed on the words *extreme case*, for it is the business of a librarian to get on rather than to get out. Some librarians under impossible conditions believe that an executive should await removal instead of resigning. On the whole a librarian, like a clergyman, serves his profession best when he keeps away from unpleasant publicity. The obvious

V. Sincerity

To delay bringing a plan before the trustees until it is certain to obtain adequate presentation and a fair hearing may be considered only common wisdom; but to abstain from urging a project until a known opponent happens to be absent is unprofessional as well as insincere.

VI. Rejected Measures

A wise librarian, when a measure has been deliberately rejected by his trustees, will not bring it forward again until new conditions prevail.

Turning now to the second of our subjects, the librarian's attitude toward those with whom he labors from day to day, we have a relationship which has been broadened and enriched by a more human understanding. This new spirit which moves on the face of the waters is the essence of the age in which we live.

VII. Duty to the Staff

A librarian is bound, as opportunity offers, to allow an assistant to prove her ability to do work of a higher character than that usually assigned to her, and to advance those that are capable to more responsible positions in his own library or elsewhere. He must also spend the money of his institution with due prudence, and get a full return for it in service. Although efficiency of the staff is temporarily reduced by frequent transfer of assistants to new positions or to other libraries, in the end a library whose workers are seen to obtain rapid and solid advancement profits by its reputation in this respect.

VIII. Performance

Having in mind that not salary but opportunity for service makes li-

remedy for this problem is for the trustees to keep their policy broad and free from detail.

This is the old question: Does the end (here the public good) justify the means? Adroitness can be cultivated to a point where it impinges upon intrigue and in that form has more than once proved a fatal accomplishment.

To see a cherished measure fail from indifference on the part of trustees or perhaps through a chance word of ridicule is hard to bear. But time is long and a librarian has need of serenity.

It might be said in reply that taxpayers do not conceive of a town library merely as a training school for other municipalities. Nor is the librarian fortunate if, after a term of years, he has lost the brightest of his staff and has retained for a lengthy old age the dull out of all those whom he has trained. Perhaps the only relief is to make the variety of work so attractive and the social opportunities so marked that members of the staff are loath to leave. The librarian should keep his staff familiar with events connected with the library in so far as these contribute to their intelligent interest in its welfare.

This canon partakes of the nature of sacrifice, but a librarian who is not at

brarianship a profession, the worker should not be too eager to move. Performance makes for dignity and influence in a community. No opportunity to serve the public can honorably be considered merely as a stepping stone or place of passage.

IX. Individual Responsibility

Each member of the staff should be regarded by the librarian as an individual, a colleague, capable of performing his particular work, and encouraged to feel his individual responsibility for this work. Where public recognition of work of outstanding merit will advance the interests of an assistant the librarian should be quick to grant it.

The wise librarian will allow to the intelligent assistant latitude in the enforcement of rules, and in their interpretation. The degree of latitude will depend on the rank and character of the assistant.

X. Recommendations

Breaches in morality and honesty are fundamental, and should be mentioned discreetly if a "recommendation" is given. Peculiarities in personality may be handicaps in one library but assets in a library of a different type. A wise librarian may mention but should not stress these, and the librarian to whom recommendations are sent will weigh so-called "defects" in the light of his own conditions and environment.

To recommend an unsatisfactory assistant, merely to get rid of that assistant, is unworthy of any administrator.

heart a missionary has chosen the wrong outlet for his energies. Under ordinary circumstances a year is the least period of service that should satisfy the conscience of an assistant.

It scarcely seems necessary to add that a librarian who has no real thought of resigning employs a doubtful expedient if he tells his trustees that he thinks of moving on unless his salary is increased.

On the other hand, assistants too often claim advancement for performing the minimum work required. It is safe to say that an assistant who habitually does more than is asked cannot be kept in obscurity.

Recommendations are an important function of a librarian's routine, and upon them careers depend for success or failure. Charity and conscience must between them determine the degree of fidelity which the portrait is to assume.

XI. The Staff's Duty to the Librarian

A librarian has a right to entire loyalty from his staff, although he may be called upon at times to face frank comment from them. Such criticism should never go beyond the library doors, nor should the staff carry complaints over the librarian's head to the trustees, except in extreme cases.

XII. The Staff's Duty to the Library

An assistant should not allow personal antagonisms within the library to injure efficiency, nor should the staff tolerate a cabal of congenial spirits that tends to break up the membership into groups ready at hand for rivalries and jealousies.

XIII. The Work and the Worker

The assistant should realize that the work is more important than the worker; that the assignment of an uncongenial task is not due to a personal grudge nor a slight to the assistant, but a necessity enforced by the work that must be done by someone.

XIV. Personal Obligation

Each assistant should realize his own personal obligation as a public servant to each library patron. He should strive always to be courteous and pleasant, remembering that the staff stands as the interpreter of the library to the public and that it may be materially helped or harmed by his individual conduct.

XV. Health

Health is an assumed qualification in a librarian's equipment, and continued ill health does not ordinarily entitle an employee to favored treatment by a public institution.

Conversely, the librarian's criticism of a member of the staff should be as private as the welfare of the library will permit. For just treatment the staff look to the librarian, and the trustee who comes between the librarian and a member of his staff lessens executive authority and in the end breaks up the morale of the entire staff.

Long periods of idleness in the case of an assistant should be called to the attention of the superior officer. Leisure has its dangers, and should be used for self-improvement as the best return for compensation received.

In the assignment of work and arrangement of schedule of hours, marked leniency toward members of long service, thereby shifting burdens to younger assistants, creates an unsatisfactory atmosphere. Long service should rarely be urged as a reason for favored treatment, nor should a low salary be advanced as an excuse for poor work.

An assistant sometimes fails to realize that some of the more desirable constituents who use the library are shy. To the mind of such a user of books the friendly assistant personifies the library. Habitual ridicule in private of mistakes or ignorance on the part of the public will affect, eventually, the conduct of the assistant.

Unfortunately the ill health of one assistant throws routine burdens on other members of the staff. It is a duty therefore to keep fit out of consideration of others. Miss Rathbone

Conversely, the library should conserve the health of the staff by furnishing the best possible equipment as regards light, air, sanitation, and rest.

says: "Far more than ever before do men today realize that health is a matter of individual achievement, the result of intelligent effort." In large libraries a medical adviser is connected with the staff and obviously has a quasi-jurisdiction over their habits of life outside of library hours. Illness in the family is not a valid claim for absence with pay. Each case must be met on its merits.

XVI. Notice of Resignation

Ethically considered, the assistant should, when seeking a change of position or when considering a definite offer from another library, consult the superior officer; but the personality of a superior officer will inevitably influence an assistant's course of action. Having accepted a position, the assistant should give adequate notice before leaving.

This subject is perhaps the most controversial of all those which are treated in these canons of ethics. It has been suggested that one's dissatisfaction should be brought to the attention of the librarian, in order that conditions may be remedied. But a mere notice that an assistant is "looking about" may result in uncomfortable personal relations lasting for several months or even years. The librarian should be careful not to prejudice himself against an assistant who desires advancement in another field of service when the right opportunity offers.

A librarian owes much to other librarians and to the professional associations, which are created for mutual benefit. We are not free lances engaged in warfare with our fellow-workers. In these relations we have:

XVII. Expert Advice

A librarian may not accept an appointment to act as an expert adviser to the trustees of another library, even when solicited, without the request, or at least without the full knowledge, of the librarian concerned.

The analogy is to be found in the physician, who may not advise a patient unless the attending physician requests it, or until the attending physician has been dismissed. At the same time there are the "survey" and the "efficiency test" that are becoming popular means of improving conditions. The expert librarian will in time take his place with the "consulting expert." It is a natural function of the leader in his profes-

XVIII. Private Advice
A librarian should feel free to claim counsel from others in the same calling, and should be willing to give such counsel when requested, without publicity or expense.

XIX. Rivalry
Librarians should be slow to publish statistics in order to show superiority of a library over neighboring libraries, such statistics often requiring qualification or explanation. A similar comparison in words is of questionable taste, and any printed criticism should always bear clearly the librarian's name.

XX. Engaging an Assistant
A librarian may not take the initiative in negotiation for the services of an assistant in another library until he has made his intention known to the assistant's superior officer; or he may make his intention known to both assistant and official superior simultaneously.

XXI. Predecessors
A librarian who makes a habit of commenting unfavorably on the work of his predecessors in office invites criticism of his good taste.

A librarian's obligation to the public exists in many forms. He needs to keep constantly before his mind that it is the *use* of knowledge rather than the storage and classification of knowledge that is the vital factor in his work.

sion. Nevertheless there must be reasonable consideration for the humbler brother of the same profession.

One of the outstanding merits of a certain librarian who was still "in harness" at the age of ninety-two was his willingness to consult men young enough to be his grandsons. Questionnaires, however, too often go beyond bounds in their call upon the librarian's time.

One can turn to annual reports of librarians which give comparative statistics with the undoubted desire to enlighten taxpayers. At the same time in so doing the librarian may embarrass other librarians who happen to be placed in a less favorable position.

Objection has been raised to consultation with a librarian over his minor assistant, but most librarians agree that before negotiations begin with an important member of another staff courtesy at least calls for a personal letter to his or her chief.

The coming of a new librarian is a strain upon the staff, and if the members are to give him their loyalty he should not speak slightingly of one to whom they have given their loyalty in the past.

The great Panizzi of the British Museum so far failed to heed the principle involved in this canon that he came very near to losing his position. He wished to do the work of a bibliographer, delegating his powers to a subordinate while he retained the honors of a head librarian. The subordinate by contact with people soon became his master.

XXII. A Librarian's Province

It is the librarian's duty to be a force in the community, and contact with people even more than with books engenders force. We must not confuse the duties of librarian and assistant; the one is always associated with people, although in a small library he (or she) may do all the work; the assistant may or may not be called upon to meet the public, but generally has specific duties to which specific hours must be given.

XXIII. Reputation

A reputation acquired by work for the public in the profession or in kindred paths of service adds to the dignity and power of the librarian. But the value of the work must advertise the worker, and self-advertising is outside the pale.

XXIV. Bearing in Public

A librarian as a person of influence, and seeking the respect of all his fellow-citizens, cannot carelessly choose his company, nor indulge in habits and taste that offend the social or moral sense. These self-limitations are in the nature of hostages which he gives for the general good. He must not limit his advisers to one circle, for he needs a wide horizon, ready sympathies, and the good will of all classes.

XXV. Use of His Name

A librarian should stand on neutral ground and should be chary of lending his name to a public controversy to add weight to the contention of a local faction, or to commercial enterprises, even those that have an educational or philanthropic motive. Having a financial interest in any material device, invention, or book proposed for purchase in his library,

Censorship of reading is a perilous No Man's Land on the boundary of a librarian's province. How far an executive should go in exposing for use books which are in his opinion destructive of morals and society, and those issued frankly as propaganda, is a serious question. The annunciation of a policy lies with a board of trustees, rather than with the librarian. Mr. H. C. Wellman in an address entitled "An Article of Faith" discusses very clearly the librarian's responsibility in the field of censorship.

A profession is like a sonnet. It confines the effort to a prescribed channel, but stimulates a higher standard of excellence within the self imposed bounds.

One may have heard a librarian say: "It is nobody's business what I do outside the library." That type of library worker has merely mistaken his calling and should change his vocation.

His advice will very naturally be sought by his constituents increasingly as his influence grows, but giving for publication a testimonial to a book is likely to lead to serious abuses. Standing on neutral ground, he should be all things to all men. "He loves all ideas—even when he despises them and disbelieves in them—for he knows that the ferthe librarian should inform his trustees of this interest. It would be better not to have a financial interest in companies whose business is largely with libraries.

XXVI. Honorarium
An honorarium for work done in library hours should not be accepted, and a librarian should be slow to undertake commissions for work outside library hours which might easily be executed in library hours without expense to the citizen.

Beyond this there is a limitless field for our canons of ethics to cover. We cannot hope to mention all the ways in which a librarian may be stimulated to high ideals. In his personal relation to books we may say:

XXVII. Book Selection
Purchases of books should reflect the needs of the community rather than the personal taste or interest of the librarian. His selection of books should be catholic, and his power to guide be exercised with discretion.

XXVIII. Specializing
The librarian should not permit specialized book collecting or book reading to narrow his field of interest, nor to bias his judgment, nor to make him a rival collector of his library. The number of points of contact with knowledge and with his public determines to some extent the librarian's usefulness.

XXIX. Relation to Agents
A librarian is bound to expend the funds intrusted to him with the best interest of the library in view. But he should remember that in employing an expert, ability and efficient service are worthy of proper compensa-

ments and chemic reactions of ideas keep the old world from growing mouldy and mildewed and effete.''

If a librarian feels impelled to add to his income by outside work it is wiser to earn by an avocation than by his vocation. Work which claims much of the librarian's strength and does not add directly or indirectly to his reputation or to that of the institution should be made known to the trustees.

A library is not a collection of books made after a fixed pattern. Each community has its bookish needs unlike those of any other community under the sun. It is this infinite variety that gives the profession which collects and makes books useful its attraction.

The fringes of all knowledge bound the administrator's province, but he, like his assistant, may by mastery of a single subject increase the renown and the usefulness of his library.

If a librarian is in doubt about the propriety of accepting a gift he should at least insist that the gift be public knowledge. Favors often come disguised in a form to flatter the unsuspecting librarian.

tion, and to sacrifice them for slightly better terms or to make frequent changes may not result to the library's permanent advantage.

He should not jeopardize his independence by accepting special favors from business firms.

XXX. Professional Spirit

The literature and the organizations of the profession claim consideration from the earnest and progressive librarian.

And in conclusion: A high professional spirit calls for sound training, clear ethical standards, and sustained enthusiasm for the fellowship of librarians. *Non ministrari sed ministrare.*[16]

In December 1929, at the ALA midwinter meeting, Josephine A. Rathbone, who then chaired the Code of Ethics Committee, presented a "Suggested Code of Ethics."[17] The committee had functioned since October 1928, when Rathbone determined the charge to the committee as: (1) determining the advisability of reprinting Bolton's 1922 canons; (2) determining if it was desirable to have a code of professional ethics; and (3) if so, preparing such a code.[18]

In her 1928 midwinter report, Rathbone had reported that the committee had concluded that Bolton's code required revision and that a revised code would be a useful guide for younger members of the profession.[19] In December 1929, when Rathbone presented the committee's version of a new code of ethics, the code was arranged around four sets of human relationships which affect a library's ability to meet the needs of its constituency. These four factors are reflected in the suggested code (printed below).

SUGGESTED CODE OF ETHICS

The library as an institution exists for the benefit of a given constituency. This may be the nation, a state, a country, a municipality, a school or college, a special field of research, industry or commerce, or some more limited group.

Libraries differ so widely in size, type of constituents, support and character of work that a code of ethics would have to be excessively detailed to apply to all situations, but certain fundamental principles may be laid down that are generally applicable.

The library's obligations relate to such collection, organization and administration of printed material or other records as will give the best possible services to its constituents. The human factors in this service are:

The trustees or other governing body or agency;
The librarian;

The staff;
The people whom the library services.

A. Governing Bodies

These may be the Board of Trustees or city officials (on whom the responsibility rests) of public or semi-public libraries; the library board or committee of college or university trustees or faculty; Board of Education or a committee thereof for school libraries or for public libraries organized under school law; officer or committee or department of a business corporation.

1. Functions

The functions of a governing body are usually prescribed by law but generally include:

The representation of the constituency for which the library exists;
The determination of the policies of the library in its service and relation to its constituency;
The exercise or delegation of the appointing and removing power;
Responsibility for bringing the needs of the library before the authorities who control appropriation of funds and for using all proper influence to get such increases as are necessary for the growth and development of the world;
The administration of the funds for the support of the library;
Responsibility for the economic, social and physical well-being of the staff, including a retirement system which is needed for the good of the service as well as of the individual.

Trustees of tax-supported public libraries, remembering that they are representatives of the whole community, should be careful not to ask special privileges for themselves or their families. The Board of Trustees should recognize that the librarian, as its executive, should attend the meetings of the board in order to be fully informed as to its desires and purposes and to aid in the formulation of its policies.

2. Appointments

The appointing power in any institution should be definitely vested in some one board, committee or person. The appointee should not consider an appointment as final unless made by the agency or person in whom that authority is lodged.

Appointments should be made for fitness only; no merely personal consideration should enter into the selection of the personnel of any library; conversely, no librarian should accept an appointment, however attractive, unless he believes that he has the ability, the training and the experience needed for ultimate success in that position, and no one should continue to hold a position unless he finds himself qualified to meet all its requirements.

3. Tenure

Having accepted a position in a library the appointee incurs certain definite obligations:

To remain long enough to repay the library for the expenditure of time and money incident to the period of adjustment; this length of time differs in different positions, but is seldom less than a year;
To remain long enough to accomplish definite results in work undertaken;
Unless a larger opportunity offer, it is best to remain in a position as long as one is able to do creative or effective work or to get satisfaction from the work; otherwise it is probably that one's usefulness in that position is at an end.

4. Resignations

Resignations should be made in writing to the authority from which the appointment came with due notification to the immediate supervisor. Adequate time should be given before the resignation takes effect for the work to be put into shape; for the appointment and, when practicable, the initiation of a successor.

5. Dismissals

Dismissals should be made whenever the good of the service demands. The employee's length of service, need of the position, and personal worthiness may be considered, but these elements should never outweigh a clear case of incompetence or incompatibility. It should be remembered that an employee who is unsatisfactory in one position may often prove effective in another department or position. Such adjustment may be attempted where practicable before dismissal. Dismissal should be made by the highest executive officer.

6. Recommendations

Trustees and librarians are sometimes dependent for information about candidates on recommendation from trustees, librarians, library schools, and other employment agencies. Recommendations should present a fair statement of the strong and weak points of the candidate.

B. Librarian
(or Chief Administrative Officer)

The librarian is the executive officer for the governing body of the library.

The position of librarian involves a threefold relation:
1. To the trustees or governing body;
2. To the constituents of the library;
3. To the staff.

1. In relation to the Board of Trustees the librarian:

Should make a loyal effort to carry out its policies;

Should make regular and systematic reports upon the work accomplished;

Should initiate plans for improvement of the service of the library;

Should act as liaison officer between the trustees and staff, interpreting each to the other and establishing, where possible, friendly relations between them.

2. Librarian and constituency

The librarian represents the library—book power and book service—and should so represent it as to win recognition for the institution rather than credit for the individual. The librarian has further obligation to the community or constituency which the library serves and should, as representative of the library (with due respect for other duties), take part in the life and activities of the community or constituency.

As representative of the library, the librarian and the staff should feel an obligation to maintain in personal conduct the dignity of the position and take care not to offend against the standards of decorum that prevail in that community or constituency.

The librarian, representing the governing body, should see that the library serves impartially all individuals, groups and elements that make up it constituency. In the case of the public library as a non-partisan institution the books purchased should represent all phases of opinion and interest rather than the personal tastes of the librarian or board members. In an official capacity, the librarian and members of the staff should not express personal, religious, or economic issues, especially those of a local nature.

3. Librarian and staff

The relations of the librarian to the staff within the library should be impersonal and absolutely impartial. The librarian owes to the members of the staff:

Stimulus to growth, to the exercise of the creative impulse, to the development of initiative and of a professional spirit;

Constructive criticism;

Freedom to achieve results and credit for such achievement;

Respect for the authority delegated to the staff;

Friendliness of attitude;

Justice in decision;

Opportunity for professional and economic advancement within that institution or some other;

Encouragement of reasonable suggestions and criticisms for the improvement of the service.

C. The Staff

1. Loyalty

Loyalty to the institution is the primary duty of all members of the staff.

Loyalty involves, in part, submergence of the individual to the institution. Such manifestations of egoism as criticism of the library or librarian outside, or the claiming of individual credit for work done as a staff member when credit should belong to the institution, are examples of disloyalty. Constructive criticism offered to the proper authority should not be considered disloyalty and should be encouraged.

Good health is a pre-requisite of good service and involves the right use of free time so that proper balance is maintained between work, recreation and rest.

The atmosphere of the library is disturbed unless the workers preserve harmony and a spirit of cooperation among themselves; hence the staff relations, while impersonal within the building, should be friendly. Envy, jealousy, or gossip should have no place in a library staff. The staff should refrain from discussion of personal affairs in the library or from attention to personal business in library time.

2. Relations to the public

The members of the staff are the interpreters of the library to the public, and its service may be materially helped or harmed by their individual contacts.

The staff owes impartial, courteous service to all persons using the library. Among the patrons entitled to use the library no distinctions of race, color, creed or condition should influence the attitude of the staff, and no favoritism should be tolerated. On the other hand, a cold officialism is to be avoided and a cordial attitude which welcomes approach should be manifested by those in direct contact with the public.

3. Department heads

Heads of departments should consider their departments in relation to the institution as a whole and never magnify unduly the importance of their own part.

Understanding and cooperation between departments is essential to the efficiency of the library's service to the community.

The heads of departments bear much the same relation to those under them that the librarian does to the library staff as a whole, and have on a smaller scale the same duties and responsibilities.

4. Assistants

Assistants are an integral part of the institution as a whole, and their suggestions for the improvement of the service should be encouraged. These suggestions should be made to the immediate superior. If differences of opinion concerning the work arise between assistants in a department, the matter in question should be taken to the head of the department for adjustment. If an assistant is critical of the policy of the department or feels that he has been unfairly dealt with, he should first discuss the matter with the head. If unable to obtain satisfaction, he may then appeal to the next higher authority. Constructive criticism or correction by responsible heads is necessary to the efficiency of any service and should be accepted by assistants without personal resentment.

The advancement of assistants should come as the result of the recommendation of heads of departments or of the librarian. Assistants should never use outside relationships to obtain a position or promotion.

The relation of staff members to the non-professional group of workers, as janitors and pages, should be strictly impersonal. Personal favors should never be asked. Their work should be directed by those assigned to the duty, and never interferred with by other staff members.

D. Library Profession

All libraries and all librarians have a duty not only to their constituents but to the profession as a whole; or to some division of it, because cooperation between libraries and librarians makes for better service to the constituents of every library. This duty involves membership and activities in one or more professional organizations, subscriptions to and the reading of professional literature, interchange of ideas and, as far as possible, of material.*

No further action appears to have been taken on the suggested code, which was printed in March 1930 and edited in 1931.[20] Committees on ethics continued to be appointed, and between 1932 and 1934, the committee chairmen reported ''no questions.'' The 1934 chairman also reported

---

*Reprinted by permission of the American Library Association from *Bulletin of the American Library Association* 24 (3):158–62 (Mar. 1930).

that attention should be called to the code through a note in the *ALA Bulletin.*[21]

In 1934, another committee was formed under the leadership of Edith M. Coulter, who served two years. In 1935, the committee reported its concern for a renewed emphasis on ethical procedures generated by the Depression and the instructions of the ALA president for coordinating the activities of the ethics committee with the Committee on Salaries and Employment. The latter had presented a resolution at the June 28, 1934, meeting of ALA in Montreal which called for a "Code of Standards for Library Services and Practice," which would include the essential personnel provisions of the 1929 code. The committee further set for itself a heavy agenda, with the goal of providing ALA Council a revised code by 1936. Its goal was admirable, but it would require more than one year to achieve. The committee further set out the need for: (1) differentiation between a code of ethics and a code of standards; (2) a code which covered specific situations; (3) organization of an educational campaign; (4) installation of machinery for making the provisions of the code effective.[22]

In 1936, Coulter's committee report was an essay in which she implied that the 1929 tentative code had lain dormant before the association. She charged ALA membership to give careful attention to "the reasons for a code of ethics"; to the "type of codes best suited to the profession"; and to a "plan of action leading to the adoption of a fundamental code."[23] She further set out criteria for defining a profession, including a formal code of ethics and an enforcement mechanism, which she indicated was the singular lack of the library profession. The plan of action by the committee included drafting modifications to make the 1929 code more specific, achieving state association adoption of the code, granting membership in the national association based on acceptance of its code, and requiring that each state have a code and be the agent for education, enforcement, interpretation, and amendment.[24]

In 1937, Flora Belle Ludington became the chairperson of a new committee which raised a series of questions that pointed to specific situations that a code of ethics should address. These questions ranged from considering the existence of essential unity in the library profession, to the consideration of impartial service provided to all patrons, to the degree to which a librarian is free to express personal opinions on controversial problems.[25] The 1938 code was an attempt to meet the needs for specificity noted by the committee since 1934 and influenced the thinking and behavior of librarians into the 1980s.

Two codes were circulated in 1938. The Junior Members Round Table published a statement on professional ethics which was prepared by the

Youngstown (Ohio) 16th Congressional District Group. This statement dealt with staff relations, staff organization, and staff responsibility. The statement was a behavioral guide which adjured loyalty, abjured use of first names among staff, referred to the library assistant in the feminine, and observed that many librarians violated rules of etiquette in vogue for sales clerks.[26]

The Code of Ethics for Librarians (printed below) was adopted on December 19, 1938, at the midwinter meeting of ALA and was printed in the *ALA Bulletin* in February 1939. The Code of Ethics Committee that produced the document was under the chairmanship of Ludington; others on the committee were John S. Cleavinger, Coit Coolidge, Edwin Sue Goree, Helen L. Purdum, Alfred Rawlinson, Rena Reese, Frank K. Walter, and Ruth Worden. This code, in 5 sections with 28 paragraphs, addressed the relationship of the librarian to a governing authority and a constituency, to staff and colleagues, and to society. In a 1939 article appearing in *Library Journal*, Louis Felix Ranlett commented on the code, supporting it but attempting to help librarians see the difference between manners and ethics.[27]

CODE OF ETHICS FOR LIBRARIANS*
PREAMBLE

1. The library as an institution exists for the benefit of a given constituency, whether it be citizens of a community, members of an educational institution, or some larger or more specialized group. Those who enter the library profession assume an obligation to maintain ethical standards of behavior in relation to the governing authority under which they work, to the library constituency, to the library as an institution and to fellow workers on the staff, to other members of the library profession, and to society in general.
2. The term librarian in this code applies to any person who is employed by a library to do work that is recognized to be professional in character according to standards established by the American Library Association.
3. This code sets forth principles of ethical behavior for the professional librarian. It is not a declaration of prerogatives nor a statement of recommended practices in specific situations.

I. Relation of the librarian to the governing authority

4. The librarian should perform his duties with realization of the fact that final jurisdiction over the administration of the library

---

*Reprinted by permission of the American Library Association from *ALA Bulletin* 33 (2): 128–30 (Feb. 1939).

rests in the officially constituted governing authority. This authority may be vested in a designated individual, or in a group such as a committee or board.

5. The chief librarian should keep the governing authority informed on professional standards and progressive action. Each librarian should be responsible for carrying out the policies of the governing authority and its appointed executives with a spirit of loyalty to the library.

6. The chief librarian should interpret decisions of the governing authority to the staff, and should act as liaison officer in maintaining friendly relations between staff members and those in authority.

7. Recommendations to the governing authority for the appointment of a staff member should be made by the chief librarian solely upon the basis of the candidate's professional and personal qualifications for the position. Continuance in service and promotion should depend upon the quality of performance, following a definite and known policy. Whenever the good of the service requires a change in personnel, timely warning should be given. If desirable adjustment cannot be made, unsatisfactory service should be terminated in accordance with the policy of the library and the rules of tenure.

8. Resolutions, petitions, and requests of a staff organization or group should be submitted through a duly appointed representative to the chief librarian. If a mutually satisfactory solution cannot be reached, the chief librarian, on request of the staff, should transmit the matter to the governing authority. The staff may further request that they be allowed to send a representative to the governing authority, in order to present their opinions.

II. Relation of the librarian to his constituency

9. The chief librarian, aided by staff members in touch with the constituency, should study the present and future needs of the library, and should acquire materials on the basis of those needs. Provision should be made for as wide a range of publications and as varied a representation of viewpoints as is consistent with the policies of the library and with the funds available.

10. It is the librarian's responsibility to make the resources and services of the library known to its potential users. Impartial service should be rendered to all who are entitled to use the library.

11. It is the librarian's obligation to treat as confidential any private information obtained through contact with library patrons.

12. The librarian should try to protect library property and to inculcate in users a sense of their responsibility for its preservation.

III. Relations of the librarian within his library

13. The chief librarian should delegate authority, encourage a sense of responsibility and initiative on the part of staff members, provide for their professional development, and appreciate good work. Staff members should be informed of the duties of their positions and the policies and problems of the library.
14. Loyalty to fellow workers and a spirit of courteous cooperation, whether between individuals or between departments, are essential to effective library service.
15. Criticism of library policies, service, and personnel should be offered only to the proper authority for the sole purpose of improvement of the library.
16. Acceptance of a position in a library incurs an obligation to remain long enough to repay the library for the expenses incident to adjustment. A contract signed or agreement made should be adhered to faithfully until it expires or is dissolved by mutual consent.
17. Resignations should be made long enough before they are to take effect to allow adequate time for the work to be put in shape and a successor appointed.
18. A librarian should never enter into a business dealing on behalf of the library which will result in personal profit.
19. A librarian should never turn the library's resources to personal use, to the detriment of services which the library renders to its patrons.

IV. Relation of the librarian to his profession

20. Librarians should recognize librarianship as an educational profession and realize that the growing effectiveness of their service is dependent upon their own development.
21. In view of the importance of ability and personality traits in library work, a librarian should encourage only those persons with suitable aptitudes to enter the library profession and should discourage the continuance in service of the unfit.
22. Recommendations should be confidential and should be fair to the candidate and the prospective employer by presenting an unbiased statement of strong and weak points.
23. Librarians should have a sincere belief and a critical interest in the library profession. They should endeavor to achieve and maintain adequate salaries and proper working conditions.
24. Formal appraisal of the policies or practices of another library should be given only upon the invitation of that library's governing authority or chief librarian.
25. Librarians, in recognizing the essential unity of their profession, should have membership in library organizations and should be ready to attend and participate in library meetings and conferences.

V. Relation of the librarian to society

26. Librarians should encourage a general realization of the value of library service and be informed concerning movements, organizations, and institutions whose aims are compatible with those of the library.
27. Librarians should participate in public and community affairs and so represent the library that it will take its place among educational, social, and cultural agencies.
28. A librarian's conduct should be such as to maintain public esteem for the library and for library work.[28]

The two decades following the 1938 adoption of a code of ethics, decades of war and recovery, and later McCarthyism, saw the adoption of the *Library Bill of Rights* and the *Freedom to Read Statement*. (The former was adopted in 1939 and amended in 1941; the current version was adopted in 1948. It has been amended in 1961 and 1967.) In 1940, the Intellectual Freedom Committee of ALA came into existence to act as an advocate for library users. The ALA joined the American Book Publishers' Council in 1953 in issuing a *Freedom to Read Statement*. These two statements became a sort of fulcrum around which the ethical concerns of librarians centered. The forces, social and political, necessary to deal with the issues reflected in the *Library Bill of Rights* and the *Freedom to Read Statement* were a reflection of the cultural and political issues of the times.

Nearly a decade after the McCarthy era, library literature again began to reflect the concern of the profession with a code of ethics. The initiative came from the Library Administration Division (LAD), which submitted the following text to the ALA Executive Board, the boards of directors of ALA divisions, the Intellectual Freedom Committee, the Committee on Accreditation, the professional staff of ALA headquarters, and the LAD officers and Executive Board. On the basis of criticism, Alphonse F. Trezza, then executive secretary of LAD, on December 16, 1960, submitted a revised document (printed below), soliciting comments. The intent of LAD was to present the final document to the ALA Council for formal adoption.

A LIBRARIAN'S CODE*

PREAMBLE. The librarian serves in one of the essential professions in a good society. He believes it is a privilege to strive toward the standards set forth in this code. He will seek to further the high purpose of libraries to make books and other records of man's experi-

---

*Reprinted by permission of the American Library Association.

ence readily accessible for the education, information, and recreation of all people. The librarian will devote his talents and energies to the cause of good library service wherever his work calls him. He will carry out his responsibilities to his governing authority and will serve his colleagues in his own library and throughout the library world. He will direct his efforts toward the betterment of library services, not only for our generation, but for generations to come.

In serving readers the librarian will promote library service which will benefit all the members of the community or organization of which he is part. He will reach out to and help as many readers as he can, and will be impartial to all.

In serving the governing authority the librarian will carry out its objectives. He will uphold the integrity of the library against any action that would compromise or weaken its usefulness.

In serving the library the librarian will place its needs and those of its readers before personal interests. He will defend the library's freedom to select for its readers the books and other materials needed for a useful and representative collection.

In serving his colleagues the librarian will respect those to whom he is responsible, those who are his fellows, and those he supervises. He will assume a fair share of the work of the library. He will reserve criticism of others for those who can act constructively on it. He will acknowledge good work by colleagues and promote harmonious relations among them. When given responsibility he will follow policies in accord with clearly stated principles in appointing, promoting, and continuing in service members of the staff.

In serving the library world the librarian will make it his duty to be a well-read, well-informed, and responsible citizen of his country and of the world. He will share in the useful activities of his community. He will work with library associations and librarians everywhere to improve library services. He will strive to achieve recognition for libraries as essential in collecting, caring for, and transmitting the recorded knowledge of our civilization.[29]

The proposal generated some discussion and action among the divisions of ALA. The Association of College & Research Libraries (ACRL) formally rejected this version of the code and published a statement written by Patricia P. Paylore.[30] Paylore's arguments reflected the librarian's allegiance to the *Library Bill of Rights,* pointed to the ineffectiveness or lack of professional impact or awareness of the 1938 code, pointed out the lack of room in the code for honest dissent, and suggested that in perpetuity the ACRL reject such codes as ineffectual devices.

The 1960/61 proposal of LAD, however, did accomplish two objectives. First, it reopened the question of the need for a code or a revision of the 1938 code. Second, it markedly altered the content and emphases of subsequently prepared and adopted codes of ethics. The initiative of LAD in 1960 apparently sparked a minor level of debate in the profession. At least, more literature appeared which addressed the question than in any other decade of the twentieth century. W.G.K. Duncan's 1961 presidential address to the Library Association of Australia, for example, is a strong statement of the ethical issues that faced librarians at the time, particularly in terms of personal and professional commitments to withstand censorship and to preserve the right to information for all citizens.[31] Duncan drew heavily on American experiences in the previous decade, particularly the *Library Bill of Rights* and the *Freedom to Read Statement*.

As part of the debate of the late 1960s, the personnel administration section of LAD, after several years' work, submitted a draft code for formal hearing at the ALA annual meeting in Kansas City in 1968.[32] The intent of the committee was to achieve ALA membership discussion and, on consideration of the suggestions received, to make modifications and send the final product to the ALA Executive Board through LAD channels. The proposed code set out "principles of ethical behavior for the library profession."[33] In its printed form, it was set out with a declaration and seven articles, each article followed by explanation. In the format below, the explanations are found in the right-hand column.

CODE OF ETHICS FOR LIBRARIANS—A DRAFT PROPOSAL

Declaration
I pledge according to my best ability and judgment that I will practice my profession with conscience and dignity; the welfare of my patrons will be my first consideration; I will respect the confidences and the responsibilities which are bestowed upon me. I will maintain the honor and the traditions of the library profession. I will not permit considerations of race, religion, nationality, party politics, personal gain, or social standing to intervene between my duty to my profession and to society. I will maintain the utmost respect for service. Even under threat I will strive for the freedom to read and for the other basic freedoms inherent in a democracy.

Article 1

The principal objective of the library profession is to render service to society with full respect for the dignity of man. The professional upholds the honor of his profession in all his actions and relations with li-

A librarian:
Recognizes and respects the worth and dignity of each individual in all procedures and actions. He is fair and impartial in the enforcement of library policies and regulations, and

brary patrons, colleagues, governing authorities of the library, and to society in general; he is always loyal to the cause of democracy and liberty.

does not give preferential consideration to any individual or group because of their special status or position in the community.

Is expected to live up to the standards of his profession and to extend its sphere of usefulness; he is alert to protect the public and his profession from those who might degrade librarianship.

Recognizes that a profession must accept responsibility for the conduct of its members and is aware that his own conduct may be regarded as representative.

Article II

The librarian carries out in good faith all policies, laws, and regulations duly adopted by the governing authorities and renders professional service to the best of his ability.

A librarian has an obligation to support the governing board and the library staff if either is unjustly accused. He should not permit himself to become involved publicly in personal criticism of board or staff members. He should be at liberty, however, to discuss differences of opinion on professional matters.

Adoption of policies and laws not in conformity with a librarian's recommendations or beliefs is not just cause for refusal by the librarian to execute these policies and laws.

A librarian will initiate action for the reconsideration or revision of a law which is inconsistent with the best interest of libraries.

If there is a situation in which a librarian feels that to retain his position would necessitate violation of what he and other members of the profession consider to be ethical conduct, he should inform the governing authorities of the untenable position.

Article III

A librarian honors the confidence and the public trust of his position.

A librarian has a commitment to his position of public trust to resist unethical demands by special interest of pressure groups or individuals. He refuses to allow unscrupulous individuals to seize or exercise powers and responsibilities which are properly his own.

A librarian respects the trust under which confidential or privileged information is exchanged in the course of executing the affairs of the library. These confidences shall be revealed only as the law or courts may require.

It is proper for a librarian to discuss confidential information with his superiors or the governing board in executive session.

Article IV

The librarian strives to provide the finest possible educational and social experiences and opportunities to all persons in his community. He seeks to improve the library program and to keep the community fully and honestly informed.

A library administrator and his staff are professionally obligated to demonstrate clear, articulate, and forceful leadership in defining the role of the library in the community, in pointing the way to achieve its functions, and in the general preservation and strengthening of libraries.

A librarian resists all attempts by vested interests to infringe upon the library program as a means of promoting their own purposes.

Article V

A librarian accepts the responsibility, throughout his career, of mastering and contributing to the growing body of specialized knowledge, concepts, and skills which characterize librarianship as a profession. Librarians should make available to their patrons and colleagues the benefits of their professional attainments.

The librarian has a responsibility to meet the educational standards recommended by his professional association and has an obligation to work toward the adoption of these professional standards by the appropriate certification authorities of his state.

Concern for improving the profession requires the librarian to seek out promising library practices and relevant research findings and to share with others any significant practices and research from within his own institution.

For the advancement of his profession, a librarian should affiliate with state, regional, and national library associations and contribute his time, energy, and means so that these associations may represent the ideals of the profession.

The ideals of the profession require that librarians support local, state, and national committees studying library problems. They should participate in such activities whenever and wherever possible, consistent with their obligations to their library.

The librarian has a professional obligation to attend conferences, meetings, seminars, and other intellectual activities which hold promise of contributing to his professional growth and development.

Article VI

A librarian applying for a position or entering into contractual agreement seeks to preserve and enhance the status and prestige of his profession.

A librarian:
Never submits official and confidential letters of appraisal for librarians or others which knowingly contain erroneous information or which knowingly fail to include pertinent data.

Provides applicants seeking information about a position with an honest description of the assignment, the conditions of work, and related matters.

Never fails to recommend those worthy of recommendation.

Exhibits ethical behavior by explaining or giving reasons to individuals affected by demotions or terminations of employment. The ability and fitness of the candidates for library positions should be the sole criteria for selection and retention.

Honors employment contracts; adheres to the conditions of a contract or to the terms of an appointment until either has been terminated legally or by mutual consent.

Does not knowingly apply for a position held by a librarian whose termination of employment is not matter of record.

Gives prompt notice of any change in availability of services, in status of application, or in change of position.

Does not misrepresent facts, use political influence or pressure tactics, nor seek to undermine the professional status of a colleague.

Does not accept or retain a position in which established principles of professional library work must be seriously compromised or abandoned.

Article VII

A librarian does not permit desire for private gain nor personal economic interest to affect the discharge of his professional responsibilities.

It is improper for a librarian to accept employment by any firm or organization which publishes, manufactures, sells, or deals in goods or services which are or may be expected to be purchased by the library system he serves.

A librarian refuses to permit his relationship with vendors primarily interested in selling goods and services to influence his work in the library system he serves.

A librarian must be cautious about using free consultative services from a commercial organization which may in reality be a technique for promoting the sale of materials in which that organization has a pecuniary interest.

It is a breach of public trust for a librarian to use confidential information about library affairs (such as the knowledge of the selection of specific library sites) for personal profit or to deliberately divulge such information to others who might so profit.

> It is inappropriate for a librarian to use unpublished materials developed by other persons in order to produce a publication for personal profit without the expressed permission of all contributors.*

In January 1970, the Code of Ethics Committee recommended a revision to the LAD Executive Board, which forwarded its recommendations to the ALA Executive Board for consideration in February 1970. The underlined portions below are those which the PAS Executive Committee suggested be deleted in January 1970.

CODE OF ETHICS (PROPOSED REVISION)†

The objective of the library profession is to serve society by the preservation, presentation and dissemination of the record of the world's knowledge, experience and aspirations. A librarian:

(1) Believes in and supports the concepts of the profession's statements on the right to read and freedom of access to knowledge and information.

(2) Up holds his profession in his actions and relations with library users, colleagues, governing authorities and with society in general.

(3) Recognizes his inter-related responsibilities to the governing authority, the constituency, to his colleagues and to society.

(4) Carries out in good faith the policies and laws of governing authorities. He will recommend, encourage and work for the adoption of laws, programs, policies and procedures consistent with the best library services and will initiate review of actions inconsistent with such services.

(5) Honors the confidence and public trust of his position. He does not permit desire for private gain nor personal economic interest to affect the discharge of his professional responsibilities.

(6) Strives to provide the most suitable educational, social, and cultural experiences to all individuals and groups in his community.

(7) Supports the work of national, regional, state and local library associations so that organizations may further the development of library service.[34]

---

*Reprinted by permission of the American Library Association from *ALA Bulletin* 62 (5) 511–14 (May 1968).

†Reprinted by permission of the American Library Association.

In November 1970, apparently in response to LAD, the ALA Executive Board established a special committee "to prepare a Code of Ethics for Librarians."[35] This committee was chaired by Margaret Monroe; other members were William S. Dix, Isobel P. Lynch, Eric Moon, and Jean-Anne South, with Ruth R. Frame acting as ALA staff liaison. In 1973, Jack Dalton was appointed chairperson; others on the committee at that time were Alex P. Allain, Jeanne Gelinas, S. Arlene Schwartz, Russell Shank, and Jean-Anne South. Ruth R. Frame continued as ALA staff liaison. This committee worked with a draft which became the basis for the statement on professional ethics adopted in 1975. Both the 1973 and the 1975 statements follow.

STATEMENT ON PROFESSIONAL ETHICS, 1973*

Introduction

The American Library Association has expressed its concern for the right and responsibilities of librarians and library patrons through its statements on intellectual freedom, the freedom to read, its *Library Bill of Rights*, and many others. Underlying these statements are certain widely held convictions upon which the members of this association agree. This statement necessarily looks toward the ideal and attempts to focus attention on certain obligations assumed by librarians. Treatment of specific areas of activity, well recognized but not dealt with here, are to be found in existing documents of the Association and will be dealt with in other documents to be issued from time to time by its Committee on Ethics.

It is true of this association, as it is increasingly true of all professions, that its individual members rarely act with that autonomy sometimes

STATEMENT ON PROFESSIONAL ETHICS, 1975*

Introduction

The American Library Association has a special concern for the free flow of information and ideas. Its views have been set forth in such policy statements as the *Library Bill of Rights* and the *Freedom to Read Statement* where it has said clearly that in addition to the generally accepted legal and ethical principles and the respect for intellectual freedom which should guide the action of every citizen, membership in the library profession carries with it special obligations and responsibilities.

Every citizen has the right as an individual to take part in public debate or to engage in social and political activity.

The only restrictions on these activities are those imposed by specific and well-publicized laws and regulations which are generally applicable. However, since personal views and activities may be inter-

---

*Reprinted by permission of the American Library Association.

wrongly believed to characterize the activities of *most* professional men and women. Indeed, one student of the subject has asserted that "in the United States, most professions are and always have been practiced in an organization by salaried employees." Whatever may be true of other professions, it seems clear that the librarian rarely acts or can act without regard to the agency of which he or she is a part, be that agency a school, college, university, public library, or private organization. Accordingly, the librarian is likely to be a member of a group with its own standards of conduct, one with procedures for dealing with matters touching its membership, or of which he or she is a part.

The American Library Association recognizes such areas of common interest and stands ready to work with other agencies whenever called upon to do so or whenever the professional conduct of one of its members is in question.

The Statement

The rights enjoyed by a citizen are in no way abridged when the professional man or woman acts as an individual in public debate or takes part in political activities where the restrictions on such activity would be those imposed by specific and well-publicized laws and regulations equally applicable to all. But it is recognized that rights involve responsibilities and that there are special obligations which devolve upon a member of this association as librarian.

The Individual

————should be aware that personal views and activities may be interpreted as representative of the institution in which one is em-

preted as representative of the institution in which a librarian is employed, proper precaution should be taken to distinguish between private actions and those one is authorized to take in the name of an institution.

The statement which follows sets forth certain ethical norms which, while not exclusive to, are basic to librarianship. It will be augmented by explanatory interpretations and additional statements as they may be needed.

The Statement

A Librarian

Has a special responsibility to maintain the principles of the *Library Bill of Rights*.

Should learn and faithfully execute the policies of the institution of which one is a part and should endeavor to change those which conflict with the spirit of the *Library Bill of Rights*.

Must protect the essential confidential relationship which exists between a library user and the library.

Must avoid any possibility of personal financial gain at the expense of the employing institution.

Has an obligation to insure equality of opportunity and fair judgement of competence in actions dealing with staff appointments, retentions, and promotions.

Has an obligation when making appraisals of the qualifications of any individual to report the facts clearly, accurately, and without prejudice, according to generally accepted guidelines concerning the disclosing of personal information.

ployed. Proper precautions should accordingly be taken to distinguish between private actions and those one is authorized to take in the name of the institution.

————may associate with any group working to attain lawful objectives. Within the limits of institutional policy one may make the informational resources of the library freely available to such groups, but one must be prepared, as a librarian, to make the same kinds of resources available, upon request, to groups holding opposing views.

The Librarian

————has a special responsibility to maintain the basic principles of the *Library Bill of Rights* whenever they are applicable to one's professional activities and the general responsibility to uphold and promote these principles, since the free flow of information is basic to the profession of librarianship.

————should seek to safeguard the essential privacy of the relationship between user and material, being careful not to divulge anything one may have learned about individual clients in the course of one's professional activities unless required to do so by competent legal authority.

————may legitimately engage in various outside activities when and as permitted by the policy of the employing institution. But one must avoid any possibility of personal financial gain at the expense of the institution.

————should seek to learn and faithfully execute the policies of the institution of which one is a part. Every staff member has the right to change existing policies by means of appropriate private or public com-

munication with those responsible
for policy decisions. If after conscientious, constructive effort the
policies of an institution continue to
be incompatible with one's own
conceptions of intellectual freedom,
justice, or library service, one may
find it ethically impossible to remain
a member of that staff.

————has an obligation to insure
equality of opportunity, provision of
adequate training and fair judgement
of competence in actions dealing
with staff appointment, retention,
and promotion. Recommendations
or decisions must not be influenced
by such considerations as race, sex,
political views, religious beliefs, or
national origins, except in those
cases in which an institution because
of particular circumstances may be
exempt from certain regulations.

————has an obligation in making
appraisals of the qualifications of a
former staff member for another
position to report the facts clearly,
accurately, and without prejudice,
according to generally accepted
guidelines concerning the divulging
of personal information.[36]

In 1975, the ALA Council established a standing committee on professional ethics, with Judith Krug as staff liaison. That committee was charged
"to augment the Statement on Professional Ethics by explanatory interpretations and additional statements, prepared by this committee or elicited
from other units of ALA."[37] This standing committee was chaired by David
Kaser and was composed of David R. Dowell, Mary V. Groner, Richard J.
Rademacher, and Anita R. Schiller. With this committee began a half-
decade of intense study and revision, which resulted in the code of ethics
adopted in 1981. At its first meeting, the committee reviewed the background to the adoption of the 1975 statement, reviewed its task, opted to
seek comments from ALA units about the 1975 statements, and declined to
endorse either the 1975 statement from the California Library Association
or the Ohio Library Association, both being considered too long to meet the
concerns of professional ethics as they were interpreted by this committee.

The committee chose to seek comments from ALA membership via *American Libraries*.[38] In the first meeting of the ALA standing committee on professional ethics may be seen the beginnings of a process through which the committee has operated and through which it has achieved eventual modification of the 1975 statement. This statement apparently was adopted by ALA Council because it was felt to be superior to the 1938 statement, but it was not one with which ALA Council felt fully comfortable.[39] This unease was not, however, identified in the minutes.

As its second meeting on July 20, 1976, the committee considered the need for hearings, and postponed consideration of hearings. It also noted correspondence from Robert E. Kemper, chairperson of the ALA Planning Committee, who indicated that the 1975 statement supported goals and objectives of ALA and that "the 1975 statement is sufficiently detailed and that any attempt to make it more specific would only detract from its usefulness."[40] Enforcement of a code was discussed; this question was one which faced the committee on repeated occasions.

At the 1977 midwinter meeting of the committee, then chaired by Richard Rademacher, the group was advised by correspondence from Frances Hatfield, chairperson of the ALA Committee on Organization, that "the Committee on Professional Ethics does have the authority under its currently approved statement of responsibility to recommend changes to Council in its basic document."[41] This clarification of authority to revise apparently set into motion the beginning of revision to the 1975 statement. At its February 1, 1977, meeting, the committee was devoted to consideration of draft statements from members of the committee, each dealing with an interpretation of one article of the 1975 statement. The committee further decided not to have hearings at the 1977 annual conference. For the next several years, the meetings of the committee reflected its preoccupation with developing a statement which, as adequately as possible, interpreted each article of the 1975 statement and proposed revisions of articles to the statement. Also, the committee began to move toward sponsoring programs at the annual ALA conferences, the first of which was at Dallas in 1979.

Through the mechanisms established to obtain commentary from ALA units and from membership, through open hearings such as the one in Chicago in 1978, and through intense discussion by the members of the committee, by 1979 the committee was ready to offer a proposal for revision of the 1975 statement. (See *American Libraries,* December 1979, p. 666. See "Draft: Statement on Professional Ethics" below.) In the October 1977 issue of *American Libraries,* the committee submitted its version of a revision of the 1975 statement.

1975 STATEMENT ON PROFESSIONAL ETHICS

Introduction

The American Library Association has a special concern for the free flow of information and ideas. Its views have been set forth in such policy statements as the *Library Bill of Rights* and the *Freedom to Read Statement* where it has said clearly that in addition to the generally accepted legal and ethical principles and the respect for intellectual freedom which should guide the action of every citizen, membership in the library profession carries with it special obligations and responsibilities.

Every citizen has the right as an individual to take part in public debate or to engage in social and political activity. The only restrictions on these activities are those imposed by specific and well-publicized laws and regulations which are generally applicable. However, since personal views and activities may be interpreted as representative of the institution in which a librarian is employed, proper precaution should be taken to distinguish between private actions and those one is authorized to take in the name of an institution.

The statement which follows sets forth certain ethical norms which, while not exclusive to, are basic to librarianship. It will be augumented by explanatory interpretations and additional statements as they may be needed.

The Statement
Indented material and bracketed words and third clause are newly suggested revisions to the 1975 Statement.

A Librarian

has a special responsibility to maintain the principles of the *Library Bill of Rights*.

> Librarianship is characterized by a variety of specializations but common to all of these is the provision of access to information. The *Library Bill of Rights,* whose very title suggests its import for the profession, concerns this function and sets forth "basic policies which should govern the services of all libraries." "Free expression and free access to ideas" and the provision of "public information and enlightenment" are central commitments of the library profession. Librarians have a special responsibility to maintain the principles embodied in the *Library Bill of Rights*.

should learn and faithfully [omit "learn and faithfully"] execute the policies of the institution [organization] of which one is a part and should endeavor to change those which conflict with the spirit of the *Library Bill of Rights*.

A librarian employed by an organization owes allegiance to the entity and not to a trustee, director, supervisor, employee, or any single person connected with that organization. In serving the organization the librarian has an obligation to learn, be able to articulate, and gain an understanding of the reasons for the policies, goals, objectives, and value system of that organization and these should be kept paramount as the librarian carries out staff activities and renders service to clients on behalf of the organization. Since a librarian must always be free to exercise professional judgment without regard to the interests or motives of other individuals, a librarian who is employed in an organization has an obligation to assess and evaluate organizational intentions. If a librarian determines that the employing institution has policies which are different from and in conflict with the spirit of the *Library Bill of Rights,* the librarian should endeavor to change those policies by constructive means in accordance with the institution's procedures established for instituting change and in accord with ethical principles. If after due time, it becomes apparent that those policies in conflict with the *Library Bill of Rights* are not going to be corrected, the librarian should no longer accept employment in that organization and professional standards should lead the librarian to expose the organization as carrying out policies in conflict with the *Library Bill of Rights.*

[should assist in maintaining the integrity and competence of the library profession.]

A basic tenet of the professional responsibility of librarians is that every person in our society should have ready access to knowledge with the help of the professional services of a librarian of integrity and competence. Maintaining the integrity and improving the competence of members of the profession to meet the highest standards of service is the ethical responsibility of every librarian. As the essence of professionalism is the delivery of quality service in response to client need, every librarian has a positive obligation to aid in the continued improvement of all phases of the profession.

must protect the essential confidential relationship which exists between a library user and the library.

As an institution for democratic living, the integrity of the library in regard to matters of privacy must be unquestionable. Right to privacy is one of the basic human rights, and abrogation of that right can only result in irreparable damage to the service ability of the library. Information which is confidential in nature consists of circulation records and professional services. Any information gained by a librarian in serving an individual is deemed confidential as in the cases of lawyers and doctors.

Confidential information may be released only under the following conditions:

Pursuant to such process, order, or subpoena as may be authorized under the authority of, and pursuant to, federal, state, or local law relating to civil, criminal, or administrative discovery procedures or legislative investigatory power. Such process, order or subpoena will be in proper form and show good cause.

Pursuant to a written request by, or with the prior written consent of, the individual to whom the record pertains.

must avoid any possibility of personal financial gain at the expense of the employing institution.

Librarians have a right to engage in renumerated activities in addition to their regular employment. Whether professional or non-professional in nature, such outside employment should not conflict with or otherwise impair performance of the librarian's ability to serve patrons objectively. The regular employer should be advised by the librarian of any outside employment which contains apparent possibilities of a conflict of interest or other impairment of the librarian's ability to perform assigned responsibilities.

has an obligation to insure equality of opportunity and fair judgment of competence in actions dealing with staff appointments, retentions, and promotions.

The failure of our society to live up to its obligations in these areas has led to legal restrictions which have recently increased our consciousness. Affirmative Action and Equal Opportunity Programs in their efforts to insure equal treatment of women and minority groups have required us to examine our procedures. Ethical standards and good practice demand that these standards be applied to all aspects of employment related decisions. These decisions must be made on the basis of valid job related criteria and not on the basis of traits that, no matter how accurately they portray the individual, have no relationship to successful job performance. This requires us to take a harder look at the requirements of the job rather than concentrate on the more easily observed personality traits and other easily observed characteristics of individuals.

Full and fair disclosure of relevant information should be the goal of all evaluations. Making this information available to the individual is part of our professional responsibility. By so doing the difficult professional judgment thus made can be instructive in assisting the career growth of the individual.

has an obligation when making appraisals of the qualifications of any individual to report the facts clearly, accurately, and without prejudice, according to generally accepted guidelines concerning the disclosing of personal information.

An ethical appraisal:

States specifically the writer's knowledge of and relationship to the individual being appraised.

Describes objectively and accurately the level of the person's positions, the competence which the applicant has exhibited, and under what different kinds of circumstances.

Does not report personal characteristics, mannerisms, physical handicaps, or illness.

Unless such handicaps or illness would directly affect (negatively) the performance of the applicant in the position for which the applicant is applying. In such a case, the letter of reference ought to state the facts objectively.

A person writing a letter of reference also has the obligation to be informed of any state regulations specifying acts of discrimination which may apply in such cases.*

Following the 1978 hearings at the Chicago midwinter meeting, the committee acknowledged three considerations in the summer of 1979:
1. Contradictory demands that the "Statement on Professional Ethics" be, on the one hand, more practical and, on the other, more ennobling;
2. Requests for revision to stress obligations to patrons;
3. Problems involved in treating the statement as a document to be enforced by the profession.

In June 1979, the committee presented ALA Council with a document labeled as a progress report. This document contained the June 26, 1979, version of a statement alongside the 1975 statement. The 1979 version was circulated in the December 1979 *American Libraries* for comment from

*Reprinted by permission of the American Library Association from *American Libraries* 8 (7): 500–01 (Oct. 1977); Copyright © 1977 by the American Library Association.

ALA membership, and a special forum was planned for June 26, 1980, in New York, to hear responses to this document. In view of the responses received to the 1979 draft statement, the committee further decided that a new statement should be prepared "which would address the issues of librarianship as viewed by the librarian *qua* librarian, not the librarian *qua* employee or administrator."[42] At this meeting, the committee accepted and edited a statement on professional responsibilities which had been submitted to it by Page Ackerman. This statement was sent to the ALA members who had responded to the proposed revision of the 1975 statement, and they were invited to the New York forum.

Fifteen persons participated in the forum in New York, and out of that experience the committee was encouraged to move directly to revise the statement on professional ethics (see draft below) and to set a reasonable goal for that achievement. To that end, Barbara Rollock, chairperson, reported to the ALA membership on June 30, 1980, the schedule under which the committee would work in order to present a revised statement to the ALA membership at the 1981 meeting.[43]

DRAFT

STATEMENT ON PROFESSIONAL ETHICS

Librarians have a special concern for the free flow of information and ideas. The American Library Association has set forth its views in such policy statements as the *Library Bill of Rights* and the *Freedom to Read Statement*, where it is clearly stated that in addition to the generally accepted legal and ethical principles and the respect for intellectual freedom which should guide the action of every citizen, membership in the library profession carries with it special obligations and responsibilities. The statement which follows sets forth certain ethical norms which are basic to librarianship.

The Statement

A Librarian

Has a special responsibility to maintain the principles of the *Library Bill of Rights*.

Should know and execute the policies of the organization of which the librarian is a part and should endeavor to change any policy which conflicts with the spirit of the *Library Bill of Rights*.

Should provide competent and complete professional service both to the individual user and to the clientele as a whole.

Should recognize and protect the user's right to privacy with respect to information sought or received and materials consulted or borrowed.

Should recognize and avoid situations in which the librarian's personal interests are served or financial benefits are gained at the expense of the employing institution.

Has an obligation to insure equality of opportunity to actions dealing with staff appointments, retentions, and promotions.*

In its meeting on February 4, 1981, the Committee on Professional Ethics reached consensus on a revised draft to be presented to ALA Council. It further instructed that wide circulation of this document parallel to the 1975 document be sought through all levels of library press, and it gave specific instructions for that implementation. At that annual conference of ALA in San Francisco, the committee affirmed the statement which had been printed in the June 1981 *American Libraries*. On June 30, 1981, chairperson Rollock reported to ALA Council the unanimous recommendation of the committee, which ALA Council accepted unanimously and referred to the July 1, 1981, membership meeting, which accepted the Council report without dissent. With that action the 1981 Code of Ethics was officially adopted by ALA membership.

STATEMENT ON PROFESSIONAL ETHICS 1981†

Introduction

Since 1939, the American Library Association has recognized the importance of codifying and making known to the public and the profession the principles which guide librarians in action. This latest revision of the Code of Ethics reflects changes in the nature of the profession and in its social and institutional environment. It should be revised and augmented as necessary.

Librarians significantly influence or control the selection, organization, preservation, and dissemination of information. In a political system grounded in an informed citizenry, librarians are members of a profession explicitly committed to intellectual freedom and the freedom of access to information. We have a special obligation to ensure the free flow of information and ideas to present and future generations.

Librarians are dependent upon one another for the bibliographical resources that enable us to provide information services, and have obligations for maintaining the highest level of personal integrity and competence.

---

*Reprinted by permission of the American Library Association from *American Libraries* 10 (10): 666 (December 1979); Copyright © 1979 by the American Library Association.
†Reprinted by permission of the American Library Association from *American Libraries* 12 (6): 335 (June 1981); Copyright © 1981 by the American Library Association.

Code of Ethics

I.   Librarians must provide the highest level of service through appropriate and usefully organized collections, fair and equitable circulation and service policies, and skillful, accurate, unbiased, and courteous responses to all requests for assistance.

II.   Librarians must resist all efforts by groups or individuals to censor library materials.

III.   Librarians must protect each user's right to privacy with respect to information sought or received, and materials consulted, borrowed, or acquired.

IV.   Librarians must adhere to the principles of due process and equality of opportunity in peer relationships and personnel actions.

V.   Librarians must distinguish clearly in their actions and statements between their personal philosophies and attitudes and those of an institution or professional body.

VI.   Librarians must avoid situations in which personal interests might be served or financial benefits gained at the expense of library users, colleagues, or the employing institution.

References

1. Charles Knowles Bolton, "The Ethics of Librarianship; A Proposal for a Revised Code," *The Annals* of the American Academy of Political and Social Science 101 (May 1922): 138ff.
2. Charles Knowles Bolton, *Library Journal* 47 (June 15, 1922): 549–50.
3. *Public Libraries* 8 (5) (May 1903): 208. From a paragraph which was a transition from the text of one speaker to Plummer's manuscript.
4. Mary W. Plummer, "The Pros and Cons of Training for Librarianship," *Public Libraries* 8 (5) (May 1903): 208.
5. Bolton, *Library Journal*, p. 550.
6. Plummer, p. 212.
7. Charles Knowles Bolton, "The Librarian's Code of Ethics," *Public Libraries* 14 (6) (June 1909): 203.
8. Genevieve M. Walton, "Library Ethics," *Public Libraries* 10 (4) (April 1905): 181.
9. Bolton, *Public Libraries*, pp. 203ff.
10. *Public Libraries* 17 (5) (May 1912): 169.
11. *ALA Bulletin* 8 (1) (January 1914): 14.
12. Lavinia B. Kirkman Penley, "Professional Ethics for Librarians from the Point of View of the Library Assistant," *California News Notes* 16 (1921): 128–31.
13. Penley, p. 128.
14. Penley, p. 131.
15. Bolton, *Annals,* p. 139.

16. Bolton, *Annals,* pp. 140ff; See also *Library Journal* 47 (June 25, 1922): 549–50 for a reference to the *Annals* and a reprint of the canons without commentary.
17. *ALA Bulletin* 24 (3) (March 1930): 158–62. (Others on the committee were Marion Horton, G. R. Lomer, Ralph Munn, Rebecca B. Rankin, and Malcolm G. Wyer.)
18. *ALA Bulletin* 23 (5) (May 1929): 120–21.
19. Ibid.
20. *ALA Bulletin* 25 (4) (April 1931): 269–70. The code was amended by the committee in 1931 and the amendments were sent to ALA Council.
21. *ALA Bulletin* 26 (3) (April 1932): 249; 27 (10) (October 1933): 458; 28 (4) (April 1934): 324.
22. *ALA Bulletin* 29 (3) (March 1935): 350.
23. *ALA Bulletin* 30 (4) (Part II) (April 1936): 368–69.
24. Ibid.
25. *ALA Bulletin* 31 (9) (September 1937): 557.
26. "Professional Ethics: A Statement for 1938," *Wilson Library Bulletin* 12 (7) (March 1938): 449–50.
27. Louis Felix Ranlett, "Librarians Have a Word for It: Ethics," *Library Journal* 64 (October 1, 1939): 738–40.
28. *ALA Bulletin* 33 (February 1939): 128–30; also 32 (9) (September 1938): 631.
29. ALA Archives, "Librarians' Code, 1960–61."
30. Patricia A. Paylore, "A Note on the Proposed 'A Librarian's Code,'" *College and Research Libraries* 22 (2) (March 1961): 163–64.
31. W. G. K. Duncan, "A Librarian's First Loyalty," *ALA Bulletin* 56 (6) (June 1962): 509–19. Reprint from the *Australian Library Journal,* October 1961.
32. *ALA Bulletin* 62 (5) (May 1968): 511–14. (Committee members were John F. Anderson, chairman, Richard B. Engen, Alice McGuire, William F. Summers, Martha Boaz.)
33. *ALA Bulletin* 62 (5) (May 1968): 125.
34. ALA Archives, "Code of Ethics Committee, 1969–70, 1973, 1975."
35. American Library Association, *Handbook of Organization 1971-72.* Chicago: ALA, 1972, p. 13.
36. ALA Archives, "Code of Ethics Committee, 1969-70, 1973, 1975;" *American Libraries* 6 (4) (April 1975): 231.
37. American Library Association, *Handbook of Organization 1975-76.* Chicago: ALA, 1976, p. 11.
38. Committee on Professional Ethics, minutes, January 20, 1976; *American Libraries* 10 (10) (December 1979): 666.
39. Ibid.
40. Ibid.
41. Committee on Professional Ethics, minutes, Frances Hatfield to Judith F. Krug, January 10, 1977, in response to Krug to Hatfield.
42. Committee on Professional Ethics, minutes, January 22, 1980.
43. Members of the committee were Barbara Rollock, Page Ackerman, Jonathan A. Lindsey, Patrick M. O'Brien, Ann E. Prentice.

Chapter 3
Commentary on the Code

The Code of Professional Ethics has been the subject of considerable discussion in the recent past; although it has been endorsed by the ALA and its divisions and by most state associations, that discussion continues. This is an indication that the code is of interest to the membership and that the process of refining its application is working. As a means of sampling current attitudes, several ALA leaders were asked to comment on the code. The following responses focus on a number of important areas: the role of the individual in adhering to the code, the need to include the code in our curriculum, and the extent to which the code can respond to the challenge of future developments in technology and services. There is concern about the lack of an enforcement mechanism; there is also concern that the code lacks inspiration.

The code will change over time and be adapted to changing circumstances; it is through discussions such as those reported here that changes will take place.

Page Ackerman

When the 1981 Statement on Professional Ethics is next revised I hope that the third sentence of paragraph two of the Introduction will be revised to read: "We, *as individuals,* have a special obligation *to use our professional skill and knowledge* to ensure the free flow of information and ideas to present and future generations [words in italic reflect proposed revision]." That change would highlight the statement's important emphasis on personal professional responsibility and its recognition of the fact that each

Page Ackerman is University Librarian Emeritus of the University of California—Los Angeles. She served on the Council of the American Library Association and was a member of the Council's Professional Ethics Committee from 1976 to 1981. Her publications include *A Study of the Needs for Research in Library and Information Science Education* and "Academic Governance and Libraries," *Library Research*, Spring 1980.

aspect of the development of collections and the organization and delivery of library and information services is an essential element in the effort to ensure that free flow of information and ideas.

The 1939 Code of Ethics reflected the then current view of the librarian as a person with special skills and responsibilities who could best serve the public interest by faithfully implementing board policies and carrying out administrative directives with competence and dispatch. The librarian was not expected to make individual ethical judgments about policy or practice in his or her library.

The 1975 Statement on Professional Ethics stressed personal professional commitment to the principles of intellectual freedom embodied in the *Library Bill of Rights* and the *Freedom to Read Statement*. It encouraged librarians to try to change institutional policies which "conflict with the spirit of the *Library Bill of Rights*" and to "learn and faithfully execute the policies of the institution of which one is a part." It also urged librarians as individuals to protect the confidentiality of the patron relationship, to ensure equal opportunity, to evaluate other individuals fairly, and to avoid conflict of interest. But the 1975 statement still did not include a statement of values or principles upon which individual librarians could make ethical judgments about functional policy and practice in the libraries they serve, nor was there any implication that they should do so.

The 1981 code tells librarians in its first section that they "must provide the highest level of service" and articulates the values by which that service is to be judged. Thus, for the first time, it fully reflects the profession's belief that librarians, in whatever capacities they serve (as board members, administrators, supervisors, catalogers, reference librarians, children's librarians, school librarians, system designers, programers, media specialists, collection developers, information managers, entrepreneurs, or consultants), acting individually or together, can and should exercise significant influence over the flow of information and ideas and that, therefore, it is important for the public interest that their professional judgments be made and their decisions and actions be taken within an explicit set of operational values subscribed to by them and known to all. Although it includes the substance of almost everything in the 1975 statement, the 1981 code omits the admonition to learn and faithfully execute the policies of one's institution—an omission designed not to relieve librarians of their ethical and legal obligations as employed persons and organization members, but to underline for everyone concerned their obligation to view themselves as participants, not passive instruments, in the complex and continuing effort "to ensure the free flow of information and ideas to present and future generations."

Caroline Arden

Although the present version of the code has its detractors, as have those codes which preceded it, it seems to me to be a strong statement of professional values and belief. I think its strength lies in its demand that the individual professional use autonomous judgment and discretion in making choices, providing equitable service, and defending the right for free inquiry. I see an even stronger aspect of the code where some of its critics see weakness; this is not merely a quixotic perversity on my part, but a considered opinion that the lack of an enforcement clause or mechanism places the responsibility on each individual to measure his or her own behavior as well as that of his or her colleagues against the standards expressed in the code. We do not leave it to a separate policing body, but we take the responsibility as individual professionals. It is a heady and heavy responsibility to be held accountable for one's own actions as well as for those of one's colleagues. It is for this reason that I should like to see a tribunal before which individuals and charges of infractions might be heard. This would be in line with the due process clause of the code and would provide a forum where questions of ethics could be examined and judged. It would be in that crucible that we could debate and refine the code as it now stands. I do not envision this tribunal as a court of law but as a professional board composed of three to five professionals, drawn from a pool of some twelve to fourteen individuals who serve staggered terms of five years each, appointed by the ALA president, and whose appointments are subject to approval by the Committee on Professional Ethics. Individuals called up before this tribunal would be represented by themselves and perhaps by one other professional colleague, not by an attorney. The accuser or accusers of the individual whose ethical behavior is under review would also be present at the hearing, after submitting charges in writing to the board and to the accused. All cases would be heard in confidence, in closed session. If, after careful hearing and due process, the charges brought were found to be true and accurate in the opinion of the ethics tribunal, then sanctions would be placed against the accused. There would be an annual report of the identities of those individuals against whom sanctions had been placed with a statement of the nature of the infraction. This report would be published but

Caroline Arden is on the faculty of the Catholic University of America in Washington, DC where she teaches ethics for librarians as part of her courses. She has worked in numerous library environments as Coordinator of Public Services for the Arlington County (VA) Public Library and as its book selection librarian, as Community Consultant to the Smithsonian Institution, as Young-Adult-Services Coordinator for Prince George's County (VA) Public Library, and as a young-adult and children's librarian. She is active in both national and regional library associations and is Virginia chapter representative to the American Library Association Council.

not broadcast by the board and would be available to any reporter for use in any publication, to any prospective employer, or to any member of the American Library Association. I believe that this peer review would give the code the added dignity of purpose and authority which it now lacks.

The foregoing dealt with an institutional means of due process which is now lacking in our present code. I should now like to turn to a most private and personal aspect of due process, one which deals with professional, sometimes personal, gossip. Gossip is always self-serving. We either tell an unverified story because it will get us attention or entertain our listeners or make us look wise and all-knowing. There is an old saying (for which I cannot, under any circumstances of "on-line" searches, verify the source) which says "burning down your neighbor's house does not make your house look any better." Our profession is a small one. We have only some 40,000 members in our most prestigious professional association, and not all of those members are professional librarians. The smaller the community, the faster "news" travels. Any good public librarian knows the truth and the fierceness of that statement.

My concern here is that we attend to three clauses of our professional code in this matter: the one which deals with due process, the one which calls upon us to separate our personal from our professional beliefs, and the one which admonishes us to be wary of any occasion which might give us pause in considering conflict of interest. I am quite aware of the *bon mot* attributed to Alice Longworth (nee Roosevelt) to the effect: "If you can't say anything nice about someone, come sit by me." It has been my experience that we, in our profession, often sit down in order to say nothing nice. It is of no importance that we say nothing or little. Listening makes us a party to the rumor. It is a very human trait to like to spread gossip. It has been my experience that in this librarians seem to be more human and less humane than most. Perhaps we are all frustrated children's librarians, or perhaps, as a group drawn to a profession which nurtures the literature of storytellers and yarn spinners, we have a collective affection for the imaginative. And we imagine all sorts of things when it comes to an unverified piece of gossip about one of our professional colleagues. We would never place an unverified citation on a scholarly document. At one time, before we succumbed to the exigencies of technological advancement, we would never have taken the title page of a monograph as the verification of an author's name. Once obituaries were carefully noted in order to "close the dates" on a catalog card. As a profession, we have been scrupulously dedicated to fact, accuracy, and detail. But it is our bent for fiction which brings us to ethical transgression. I am sure that most of us can recall instances where professional reputations and, subsequently, careers have been hampered and sometimes demolished by caluminous gossip. No one wants to appear to be "holier than thou" or self-righteous; I think it is this desire which often prevents us from squelching a rumor or questioning a juicy tale. Here once more we see the self-serving aspect of gossip at work. Sometimes we will listen without comment in order to give the appearance of going along with the group or we may remain silent and not question out of fear of antagonizing the gossiper who may, in a fit of pique at having had a story ruined, turn the malicious tongue on us. No matter how we look at it or try to rationalize it, indulging in gossip about our colleagues, whether actively or passively, is a gross violation of our professional ethic. Any system of professional ethics calls upon us to reconcile self-love with love of duty. It is in the realm of gossip that this demand is most keenly felt.

Lester Asheim

The importance of a code of ethics as the basis for professional performance is—to me—unquestionable. But as many other commentators on ALA's code of ethics have noted, ours seems to lack the inspirational tone that would fire the imagination of librarians and strengthen their resolve to carry out its precepts. Maybe "precept" is the problem: In my desk dictionary, one of the meanings of the word is "an order issued by legally constituted authority to a subordinate official," and I'm afraid that the ALA code conveys that tone. What I wish the code could do—and I don't know how to restate it to make it do so—is clarify principles to which we would wholeheartedly desire to adhere, rather than to prescribe actions we must (or must not) take.

I guess part of my problem is the consistent use of the verb "must," which tells us what to do instead of identifying the purpose served. Would it help to see us as dedicated to the promotion of freedom of access and freedom of choice for all persons, instead of being told we must resist all efforts to censor (where the very meaning of "censor" is subject to a variety of interpretations)? Or to underline the library's special role in promotion of equality for all persons, instead of "must adhere to the principles of due process"?

Lester Asheim is William Rand Kenan, Jr., Professor of Library Science at the University of North Carolina—Chapel Hill. Prior to that he was on the faculty of the Graduate Library School of the University of Chicago and from 1952 to 1961 was Dean of the school. He served on the staff of the American Library Association as Director of the Office for Library Education from 1966 to 1971 and as Director of the International Relations Office from 1961 to 1966. He has received numerous awards in recognition of his service to librarianship, including the Joseph W. Lippincott Award in 1976, the Beta Phi Mu Award in 1973, and the Scarecrow Press Award for Library Literature in 1973.

I realize that the Introduction tries to do this and that the code tells us how, but somehow the code seems cut and dried, not a spontaneous response to ethical considerations.

As I read this over, I seem to be suggesting that we should have a code, but we should not try to codify it.

Jack Dalton

Any discussion of a code of ethics for the American Library Association today must rest firmly upon a large number of position statements and policy statements adopted by the association through the years, most particularly upon the *Library Bill of Rights* (1948), the *Freedom to Read Statement* (1953), and the amendments to both. These two documents say so much so well that they ought to be printed in each edition of the *ALA Yearbook*. We do tend to forget what we have said.

I have before me as I write the ALA's Statement of Professional Ethics, 1975 and various drafts prepared since that was published. That statement has been steadily improved upon, but all the drafts from 1975 through 1981 cover the same topics—censorship, conflict of interest, the individual's right to privacy, equality of opportunity, and access to information—while giving obeisance to the two documents already mentioned and while urging librarians to "distinguish clearly in their actions and statements between their personal philosophies and attitudes and those of an institution or professional body." These same points are all covered, either explicitly or implicitly, in the *Library Bill of Rights* and the *Freedom to Read Statement* or in the various amendments to these documents.

The efforts of successive groups over the past 35 years to codify our ethical standards, usually under an injunction to "make it brief," have involved us in the difficult task of reducing some lengthy and closely reasoned arguments to a few rules of thumb while at the same time attempting to produce a statement that will prove acceptable to a wide variety of librarians in all sorts of libraries. Can this be done? Remembering the debates through the years over the futility of codes without sanctions

---

Jack Dalton is former Dean of the School of Library Service of Columbia University. He was Librarian of the University of Virginia from 1950 to 1956 and from 1956 to 1959 was Director of the International Relations Office of the American Library Association. After his service as Dean at Columbia in 1970, he became Director of Columbia's Library Development Center, an office established under a Rockefeller grant to survey library service to the economically deprived, the physically handicapped, and others isolated from library service. He has long been concerned with the role of a code of ethics for librarians and has in many ways contributed to its development. In 1983 he received the highest award of the American Library Association, honorary life membership, in recognition of his "incalculable contributions to American librarianship."

and the discussions of whether ALA is in a position to police the violations of *any* code, one has to wonder.

Is it quibbling to suggest that what was a statement cannot be transformed into a code by simply changing its name? And is it nit-picking to suggest that those who have suggested that without sanctions a code is meaningless may have a point?

The group that was asked to consider these matters in the early 1970s pondered these and many similar questions, held hearings on two different occasions at summer conferences, and examined many codes of ethics and statements on ethical responsibilities and obligations, an exercise repeated many times in the past 35 years by many different ALA groups. In its search for organizations most like ours in their composition and operations, ALA agreed that the Association of American University Professors (AAUP) came closest, and it was impressed, as it reported to the ALA Council, by AAUP's decision to issue a statement rather than present a code with the intention of issuing "from time to time supplemental statements on specific problems." (Isn't it about time for ALA to issue some kind of statement on the librarian and his/her computer?) It also agreed with AAUP that "in the enforcement of ethical standards the [library] profession differs from those of law and medicine, whose associations act to insure the integrity of members engaged in private practice."

That group felt that in proposing a standing committee on ethics to replace the ad hoc committee, of which it was the latest in a series, it was proposing machinery for exploring such differences as well as such problems as might arise from time to time. It had no doubt that in time ALA would decide it needed a code and would provide such mechanisms as such a code might require. Question: Have we arrived at that time?

Brooke Sheldon

Rather than discuss any specific aspect of the code itself, I'd like to mention a matter which some may disclaim as trivial but which is a pet peeve related to ethics. There is an area in which I feel that my colleagues in top and middle management, who otherwise are totally ethical, are often flagrantly guilty of breaking the code.

I believe that when a person who is filling a vacancy asks for a reference regarding an applicant, that person has a right to expect an honest

Brooke Sheldon is Dean of the School of Library Science at Texas Woman's University. She has served on the staff of both the Alaska State Library and the New Mexico State Library and was Director of the Leadership Training Institute at Florida State University. She has been active in both state and regional library associations and served as President of the American Library Association from 1983 to 1984. Her publications deal with interlibrary cooperation and management.

response. For some reason, members of our profession who would never lie otherwise have absolutely no hesitation in supplying a glowing recommendation even when a person is known to be totally incompetent. Thus, a person who is lazy and lethargic becomes "good-natured" and "easygoing"; a person who is surly and finicky becomes "introspective" and "pays attention to detail." Now, I'm not suggesting that persons should not be given the benefit of a doubt, and that different situations bring out different talents, but we do both the employer and the employee a disservice when we try to portray a dud as a diamond. On the other hand, we need to be equally sensitive to the possibility that personal prejudices or relationships can interfere with an evaluation of a person's potential.

A librarian's evaluation of a colleague ought to be a statement in which trust can be placed. We owe this to each other and to our institutions.

Robert Vosper

We have been rather slow to develop a modern code of ethics pointed at the librarian's responsibilities to library users and to the profession rather than indicating a self-centered concern for protecting the rights of librarians. Now that we have one, though, a next order of business must be to establish a procedure for sanctions against librarians who breach the code. Toward that end we must assure both students and practitioners, as well as the public, that the code is not simply an abstract statement but a statement of best practice. One hopes that this book will aid in such an educational effort.

To be sure, we have not been alone as a profession in so recently facing up publicly to our ethical responsibilities. Our recent change of face and of pace in this regard fits into a trend of the recent past, whereby most of the established professions have given greater emphasis to questions of ethics and to the teaching of ethics. They have done so, no doubt, in response to societal pressure stemming from the Watergate years and increasing public skepticism during the 1970s about professional privilege. The rapid rise in medical malpractice suits is but one dramatic indication of this public distemper. Thus, our 1981 restatement fits into a general social pattern that we must take seriously.

It has been asserted that, whereas in 1979 almost every medical school had an ethics course, five years earlier there were almost none. In 1976, the

Robert Vosper is Emeritus University Librarian and Emeritus Professor at University of California—Los Angeles. He served on the American Library Association Council from 1960 to 1972 and was President of the American Library Association from 1965 to 1966. His extensive publications deal with acquisitions, collection development, and national and international library planning. He has been honored for his service to librarianship by the Guggenheim Foundation and by the government of Belgium.

distinguished Wharton School instituted a business ethics course, the professor of which felt that ''we (in business) have been slow in trying to teach ethics in the classroom.'' The California Bar Examiners in 1975 for the first time included a test of legal ethics in the statewide bar examination, and 44.2 percent of the would-be lawyers failed this section on professional responsibility. During this same period in the mid-1970s, other professions, including accounting, engineering, public administration, and journalism, began to offer ethics courses, according to a 1979 news report from the American Philosophical Association.

I wish I knew more about our own teaching of ethics. A recent analysis done at UCLA of courses offered in library schools revealed that no school lists a course on ethics. This does not surprise me in view of the shortness of our training programs, but I was surprised to learn that apparently no school offers a course in intellectual freedom, which of course is at the heart of our ethics. To be sure, it is likely that these matters are dealt with to one degree or another in courses labeled Introduction to Librarianship, The Library in Society, and the like; an important question, though, is: Should we be doing better for our students in this regard, in view of the general trend in the professions?

In terms of our new code it is also of interest that in 1978 the British Library Association set up a Working Party on Professional Ethics which in 1980 issued a Draft Code of Professional Ethics, the first overt British move in this field. The subsequent widespread and intense discussion led to the adoption by membership in September 1983 of an official Code of Professional Conduct; notice the change in terminology. Although more detailed than our 1981 statement, the British code affirms most of the same principles. However, the British go an important step further in authorizing a disciplinary committee to admonish, to suspend, or even to expel from Library Association membership any librarian failing to comply with the requirements of the new code, a critical matter under the British system of chartering librarians. They obviously mean what they say in their code. Do we?

Robert Wedgeworth

In my discussions with students and younger members of the profession, I find it useful to remind them of their professional status based upon a

---

Robert Wedgeworth served as Executive Director of the American Library Association from 1972 to 1985. He has served on many committees, including the National Library of Medicine Biomedical Library Review Committee, the Library of Congress Network Advisory Committee, the Executive Committee of the Center for the Book of the Library of Congress, and the Board of Visitors of the University of Pittsburgh Graduate School of Library and Information Science. His credits include the editorship of the *ALA Yearbook* and the *ALA World Encyclopedia of Librarianship*.

long history of professional practice and an organized body of guidelines and principles. Since 1981, we have also promulgated a statement of professional ethics which guides our long-term professional aspirations and makes librarianship more than just another job.

The six principles that constitute the ALA Code of Ethics deserve much more prominence, as they give librarians a prominent place among all information workers moving into the information age.

It will be these principles that will be sorely tested as we develop new products and services, as we define who will be eligible for various services in libraries and other information-providing agencies, and as we determine what materials will be available for use. These are not trivial questions, for they have troubled librarians throughout the years in terms of dealing with difficult formats, in terms of combating censors, and in terms of relating to many different kinds of people, some of whom have behavioral customs and languages that are totally unfamiliar.

These will be fundamental challenges for librarians and other information workers in the future, and a strong statement of professional ethics can certainly be of assistance in guiding the development of how librarians respond to these situations.

William J. Welsh

The only justification for a code of ethics for any given profession is to protect the public. The code of ethics adopted by the Council of the American Library Association has been drafted to protect the library's particular clientele from unprofessional conduct. The code, as drafted, serves as a reminder to the librarian that librarianship is a high calling demanding professional conduct and, on certain occasions, great personal sacrifice.

I will attempt to apply the code of ethics to service at the Library of Congress. Our librarians are called on to serve Congress, the government, scholarship, other libraries, and the general public. In fulfilling this mission it is essential that the collections of the Library of Congress are usefully organized, that our circulation and service policies be guided by a clear mission statement, and that all publics, be they members of Congress or citizens requesting information in any one of our reading rooms, receive accurate, unbiased, and courteous responses.

William J. Welsh has served as Deputy Librarian of Congress since 1976. He has written and lectured widely on library administration, the governance of library networks, and the application of technology to preservation of materials. He has been active in the American Library Association and the Council on Library Resources. In 1971, he received the Melvil Dewey Award.

The Library of Congress has a national responsibility to collect materials on all subjects of research value, be they for now or for centuries to come. It would be unconscionable for the Library of Congress as a beacon of a free society to submit to any national or political pressure in its collection policies. Fortunately for the nation, few instances of such pressure have arisen in the library's 184-year history, and the library has become the greatest repository of knowledge in the world.

As a parliamentary and national library serving those who shape national policies, it is inherent in our free system of government that the Library of Congress's circulation records not be subject to inspection by the public, press, or by a governmental entity.

Library of Congress personnel, practices, and policies provide due process and equal opportunity to all of its employees as well as to potential applicants. It is essential that our librarians distinguish clearly their personal pronouncements and philosophies from those of the Library of Congress, whose mission is to provide nonpartisan, accurate, and full information to those serving in the Congress and the government and to the general public. All employees in the federal sector are prohibited by law from actions in which personal interest might be served or financial benefits gained at the expense of the public or the employing institution.

The code of ethics serves to protect the public in gaining equal access to library resources of this nation, thus ensuring that the fundamental principles on which this nation was founded are respected.

Robert Oppenheimer, in *Science and Common Understanding,* summed up what we are about when he said: "The open society, the unrestricted access to knowledge, the unplanned and uninhibited association of men for its furtherance—these are what may make a most complex, ever growing, ever changing, even more specialized and expert technological world, nevertheless a world of human community."

Virginia G. Young

The Code of Professional Ethics for librarians is an excellent statement of the power and responsibility, as well as problem areas, faced by all librarians. Librarians and their governing boards can serve their libraries well by the adoption of and adherence to this code of ethics. It should be

Virginia G. Young has been active as a library trustee and community leader nationally as well as in her home state of Missouri. She was an early supporter of the White House Conference on Libraries and Information Service and served on its planning committee. She has been active in the American Library Trustee Association, serving as its President from 1959 to 1961 and on numerous committees. She has served on the Carnegie Foundation for the Advancement of Teaching Committee on Governance and Higher Education since 1977 and on the board of the League of Women Voters of Missouri. Her publication *The Library Trustee* serves as a guide to trustees nationwide.

given wide publicity to increase the public awareness and understanding of the importance of the library and the profession. It can help focus attention on how central the library is to our way of life through intellectual freedom and freedom to access.

The first four articles of the code are very positive, objective statements which clearly delineate the librarian's role with regard to the employing institution and the community served. Articles five and six, although clearly stated, still cover areas where individual subjectivity comes into play and will continue to be areas in which problems are most likely to arise.

It requires real effort and soul-searching, for example, to "distinguish clearly" between one's "personal philosophies and attitudes and those of an institution or professional body." Without extreme care, it is very easy to exert influence upon a library collection and a service program by commission as well as omission. Policies established in concert with the board of trustees and director will help give the objectivity needed that could not be achieved alone.

The last two articles, however, inspire personal integrity. The code, of course, will be workable to the degree that the local librarian interprets it in the spirit in which it was written.

The code holds the standards of librarianship high. Public knowledge of this code is an opportunity for people to salute librarians' achievement in seeing that our libraries are truly the bulwark of our democracy.

Chapter 4
Cases and Questions

Questions of morality and ethics do not arise in a vacuum. They arise from the experience of persons who are responsible participants in civic, cultural, and professional life. They often arise because the sense of right on which an individual has operated has been perceived to have been violated, and from that sense of personal concern the broader question has been raised. As one analyzes American library history, one cannot avoid being aware of the focus of social concerns which developed in American culture during the mid- and late 1960s. As a result of the concerns that developed those years, all of American culture focused on a single series of events in terms of a phase of ethics and morality—Watergate. But for librarians an event prior to Watergate focused attention on social and ethical questions in a new way; the 1969 Annual Conference at Atlantic City is generally viewed in library circles as a pivotal event. The end result, at least historically, of that conference was to focus questions of social responsibility into a new level of consciousness for librarians. At the base of questions of social responsibility are questions relating to ethics.

Although it would be difficult to demonstrate a causal relationship, we can acknowledge that out of the fulcrum of social concerns confronted by librarians and the social responsibility for the profession as a whole and individually, a change occurred in the nature of the ethics statements of the American Library Association. From 1903 until the push by the Library Administration Division to raise the question of a code in the 1960s, librarians' ethical statements had been based on a prescriptive, behavior-oriented foundation. In the 1960s, in their statements of professional responsibility and ethics, librarians moved toward an approach that provided a foundation for the development of behavior (morality) but was not behaviorally prescriptive. This approach may be more difficult to deal with, but it is probably more appropriate for a pluralistic culture such as our own. When behavior is prescribed, the moral issues appear (or tend to

appear) in sharper focus. When behavior is derived from an ethical principle, individual judgment is part of the moral picture. The 1981 ALA Code
of Ethics can be seen as a foundation that requires interpretation.

The Professional Ethics Committee of the American Library Association recognized the role of interpretation and, in 1977, published comments
on the articles of the code of professional ethics that was operative at that
time. As the committee worked through the 1975 statement and decided to
recommend a new statement in 1981, it again approached the question of
interpretation. To that end the committee sponsored a program at the annual
meeting in San Francisco at which it presented case studies for comment
and interpretation. The approach of the committee was to demonstrate that
the code applied to the case in question and to identify what portion of the
code applied. In this manner it sought to begin the process of educating the
membership about the impact of the code. The cases presented by the
committee in 1981 were:

I.   Rev. John Smith is the chairperson of the public library
        board in a medium-sized town (pop. 50,000). He is also the
        minister of a large local unaffiliated church whose members
        have become concerned about morality and the spread of
        allegedly pornographic literature in the area. Recently the
        Board of Deacons, the governing body of Rev. Smith's
        church and his legal employer, voted unanimously to
        endorse and actively pursue a campaign to remove several
        controversial titles from the library. The deacons appear to
        have the support of the overwhelming majority of Rev.
        Smith's congregation.
            While Rev. Smith himself is critical of the books in
        question, he also opposes censorship. Indeed, it was Rev.
        Smith who convinced the library board to endorse the
        Library Bill of Rights, and in meetings with deacons he has
        attempted to dissuade them from supporting the book re-
        moval drive. As chairperson of the library board, Rev.
        Smith feels obliged to implement the intellectual freedom
        policies which he approved in the past; in fact, many board
        members will be counting on him as their most articulate and
        prestigious spokesperson. On the other hand, his obligation
        as minister is, according to the practices of his denomination,
        to support the deacons, and he has good reason to fear he will
        be dismissed from his ministerial position if he fails to do so.

II.   Rushmore Studios, a producer of film documentaries, has
        become aware of libraries' interest in films. As a matter of
        fact, the school and library market is responsible for the
        majority of their sales, and the majority of the
        distribution of their productions on a national scale is
        to libraries. Their short film subjects represent a

quality product in the film world and libraries throughout the country have used these films widely for programs, including discussion groups, senior citizens' programs, in-service training, film workshops, etc.

The president of Rushmore recently approached a division of ALA with a proposal to create a film award he would willingly support with a substantial cash advance. Films in several categories, would be eligible for the award including documentaries.

The committee assigned to study the proposal noted that the majority of the documentary films were produced by Rushmore Studios and felt that the award in this category would most certainly go to Rushmore Studios because of its superiority over other filmmakers in this area.

Rushmore Studios did not offer to remove their films from the competition with other companies when awards were being considered.

Some members of the division felt that unless Rushmore films were eliminated from the competition, financial backing for a film award was not acceptable.

III.   Dale R. is a collector of first editions of the works of Ralph Waldo Emerson and has, over the past eight years, put together a collection that, although not extensive, is respectable and gives its owner a measure of satisfaction. Dale R. is also head of special collections for Saxtons College, a medium-sized liberal arts institution with a solid academic reputation. On a fairly regular basis, in his role as head of special collections, Dale is informed of the anticipated availability of materials appropriate to the college's collection development priorities. Recently, a copy of Emerson's *Essays* was included in a list of materials to be sold from the estate of a well-respected collector of Americana. It would be a useful addition to the college's collection. It was also an item Dale R. had long hoped to own. Available acquisition funds would not allow the library to purchase the total collection available for sale. A number of items could be purchased for the library and their purchase justified. The Emerson item would fit well into Dale's personal collection. At a private sale where the individual purchasing on behalf of the library knows of materials available which would be of personal interest as well as of value to the library's collection, should that individual purchase only for the library's collection?

IV.   Your library spent six months preparing bid specifications for an automated circulation system. In addition, during the past years, your board has put over $0.5 million into a capital fund. Thirteen companies have responded to the bid and all but two are within $25,000 of your projected estimate. Your board is not restricted to bid procedure by law, but as a matter of course usually operates on a "lowest and best" bid basis.

Your evaluation team, which included several data processing experts from local large companes, has determined that six of the lower bidders and the two higher bidders all responded in accord with the requirements. One of the high bidders and one of the low bidders, however, have no circulation system in operation at present. Both of these companies rank at the bottom of the acceptable list. Your recommendation to the board is to go with one of the top low bidders because you have had favorable responses on that company from a telephone survey you conducted with other library directors.

The bottom ranked higher bidder is a local corporation on whose board two of your board members formerly sat. In committee, they convince their library board colleagues to award the bid to that company, claiming they no longer have any financial interest. The library board committee votes to make the award and overrules your recommendations. You have one week between the committee meeting and the formal board meeting at which they will make the recommendation. The money difference between your recommendation and theirs is $80,000. What, if anything, do you do to stop this seeming overexpenditure of taxpayer's dollars?

V.   Ms. X, a member of a self-perpetuating library board of trustees, declared her availability for paid employment after having completed a post-graduate course of studies in statistics, a field she originally studied prior to rearing her family. The president of the board, having observed Ms. X's capabilities not only on the board but in various other voluntary agencies in the community, suggested she fill a current vacancy as a library comptroller. Ms. X finds the monthly trustees meeting for which she receives no remuneration quite satisfying and feels that the committee on sites and buildings which she chairs would prove no deterrent to the pursuit of her paid job as library comptroller. Members of the staff contend her retention on the board of trustees constitutes a conflict of interest since the comptroller's position is under the jurisdiction of the board.

Other professional groups raise ethical questions that can apply to librarians. The International City managers Association asked its constituency "Are You an Ethical Public Employee?" through a set of 10 "common ethical dilemmas."[1] Since librarians are primarily public employees, these ethical dilemmas may be of interest. The 10 situations were developed by Sheldon S. Steinberg, University Research Corporation, and tested in a series of workshops. The situations provide for a "yes/no" response, with the responses weighted on a 1–3 scale. The 10 questions deal with realistic situations that may be faced by public employees. They include

1. being a guest at the annual chamber of commerce weekend outing;
2. accepting an honorarium for speaking to a group of officials from another city;
3. potential conflict of interest in continuing an established social relationship when one party may appear to benefit financially;
4. accepting offer of free coffee from local restaurant owner;
5. promoting a respected and conscientious employee who reported misuse of city automobiles;
6. pressure from a developer to have you represent him in a transaction which would give him a zoning benefit;
7. receiving expensive gifts from a large corporation;
8. keeping a fifth of premium brand liquor found in your sack when you got home from the liquor store;
9. investing in a building with a group from which you could realize a significant profit in a city in which you are the city manager; and
10. a long-term, reliable and responsible staff member confesses to "borrowing" from petty cash, but repaying it, and personnel policy would call for termination.

Not only public administration but also the science and technology fields provide ethical questions and cases. Donn B. Parker provided 47 scenarios in *Ethical Conflict in Computer Science and Technology: Workbook,*[2] the product of a National Science Grant. Because of the impact of technology on libraries, the scenarios that Parker identified in his workbook are important for librarians. One scenario (2.10) in particular is beneficial for librarians who are in the process of purchasing computer hardware. The case, which follows, deals with the obligation of the dealer to provide documentation for the operation of the system. How careful should the librarian be to assure that adequate documentation is available, and what recourse has the librarian when a contracted obligation is not honored? What is the ethical question from the perspective of the librarian and from the perspective of the hardware vendor?

SALES MANAGER, TURNKEY MINICOMPUTER SYSTEM: INTENTIONALLY PROVIDING SCANT DOCUMENTATION

A first-time user contracts to buy a minicomputer, complete with all programs and training needed for his order processing, billing, sales analysis, inventory control, and accounts receivable functions. The vendor performs as agreed, developing customer application programs specifically for this user, but the sales manager intentionally provides only sketchy documentation, so that he will have a captive customer for program maintenance. The user then requests thorough documentation and offers to pay the incremental costs, explaining that he plans to hire a staff member to maintain these programs and develop new ones. The sales manager refuses to provide more documentation under any circumstances. The original agreement required the vendor to provide "all documentation required to operate the system."

Questions are often easier to generate than case studies. Below are some questions which have been discussed by the ALA Professional Ethics Committee between 1980 and 1984. The questions in their original form were generated from a variety of sources, including representatives from other ALA divisions during a 2½ year period when the Professional Ethics Committee held working sessions in an effort to broaden awareness of ethical concerns.

1. Accuracy and timeliness of information in three sensitive areas generate concern about personal liability for librarians. The areas are medical information, legal information, and business information. To what extent is the librarian personally responsible for the accuracy of the data to which the librarian may direct or provide a patron? Do medical and legal librarians operate under a code of ethics or a system of behavior which is different from other librarians?

2. A library patron has need for paint wholesale prices and the data are not easily or generally available in public sources. The librarian, however, through personal relationships, can obtain the data. What is the ethical use of the data gained in this manner? Does this kind of data gathering/dissemination differ from the earlier percepts of the role and function of the librarian as an information disseminator?

3. If library books are found at a crime scene and police wish to identify the person who circulated the books, what ethical concerns ought the librarian address in the process of providing or not providing the information? How does the librarian appropriately differentiate ethical and legal questions and responsibilities? To what extent and on what basis are circulation data confidential?

4. In a college/university reserve room, has the faculty the right to examine circulation data to determine which students have been performing reserve reading?

5. In a political district which has a "dry" alcohol policy, is it ethical for the librarian to order for circulation a book on wine making?

6. What personal privileges, i.e., circulation, should be exercised by library staff? How about other personal perquisites such as no fines, etc?

7. Is it ethical for a library school faculty member to require students to purchase a text which that faculty member has written?

8. What is the real violation when an author/publisher reprints an article without notifying the writer of the article if the writer does not own copyright?

9. Is it ethical to submit the same article to more than one publisher simultaneously?

10. Is it ethical for a prospective employer to require salary data from previous employments?

11. Are there differences between business ethics and librarians' ethics? What are these differences, and how do they affect the functioning of librarians?

12. How does a librarian differentiate between personal ethics, professional ethics, and public responsibility? Is there potential conflict among these?

13. In bid systems what are the ethical issues in:
    a. giving a contract to a personal friend who has a higher bid;
    b. specification writing by potential bidder;
    c. demonstrating equivalency when "or equivalent" is a term in the bid specification (i.e., is equivalency demonstrated by vendor or initiator)?

14. Is the professional judgment of a librarian who accepts no vendor entertainment invitations at a higher ethical level than the professional judgment of the librarian who accepts vendor invitations?

15. A department in a university is facing accreditation by its professional agency, and library holdings are a criterion. Differentiate the conflict of interest and ethical questions which may be faced by the librarian and the department head concerning the collection and its management in relation to the endorsement of the discipline. For instance, retaining holdings for volume count without regard to use. Others?

16. What are the ethical questions in establishing a "permanent reserve" for items which may be sexually graphic in presentation? Are these concerns addressed in the 1981 statement of professional ethics for librarians?
17. Identify the ethical questions which a librarian must face in dealing with perceived (or acknowledged) professional incompetence.

Another product of the Professional Ethics Committee liaison with divisions to raise awareness of ethical issues came about in 1983 when the Professional Ethics Committee asked Art Plotnik, the editor of *American Libraries*, to provide an opportunity for ethical questions to be raised and responded to by the membership through the publication. The first two questions came from individuals in the profession, and the responses followed directly.

1. A patron requests an auto repair manual, then asks the librarian to name a good mechanic. The librarian knows one, but is it proper to offer a name? (*AL*, February 1983, p. 79; responses, *AL*, May 1983, p. 270)
2. What is the legitimate extent to which a library director might "approve" employees' journal articles and correspondence for professional associations? (*AL*, May 1983, p. 271; responses *AL*, July/August 1983, p. 452)

As ALA membership generates questions, Plotnik will provide space for the questions and for responses.

In 1976, as a stimulus to the committee that was appointed by the Council following the adoption of the 1975 statement of professional ethics, chairperson David Kaser posed 17 questions. Sixteen of these questions are still relevant, and the seventeenth is irrelevant only because it refers to articles in the 1975 statement which were not retained in the 1981 statement. Kaser's questions, recorded in the minutes of July 20, 1976, are provocative.

1. A journal was directed by court order to warn libraries that "it may be a crime" for them to circulate or make available information which was contained in one of the journal's articles. What should a library do under such circumstances?
2. In three successive years a library's budget authority has deleted a specific line from the library's budget which would have made funds available "for continuing education of staff." Can the library justify paying for some continuing education out of other related budget lines, such as "Travel" or "Supply & Expense"?

3. Can librarians serving on state committees for library development rationalize the recommending of grants to their own libraries?

4. If we assume that the relationship between a librarian and a client is confidential, what is the proper action for the librarian who is asked for assistance on a research problem which he knows is being investigated by another researcher to whom the librarian also owes confidentiality? Not to violate confidentiality will lead to duplication of research effort.

5. A member of a neighboring community seeks assistance from an adjacent library in proving that the patron's own librarian is censoring the book collection. Is it ethical to aid him in this effort?

6. Is there cause for a library to refuse to hire librarians into paraprofessional or clerical positions? What about terminating persons from such positions once they have taken library degrees?

7. At what point does the reliance of a small library upon the larger resources of a neighboring institution cease being judicious cooperation and become unethical ''free-loading''?

8. Is the responsibility of a library to reply to inquiries about employment a courtesy or an ethical obligation?

9. What is to be done by the library administrator who is informed by a junior clerk in the office of a book supplier that the supplier and the acquisitions librarian are falsifying invoices? The clerk has furnished evidence on condition that his identity not be revealed because he does not want to lose his job with the supplier, thus debarring the administrator from bringing charges which could lead to dismissal of the acquisitions librarian.

10. Two independent libraries exist in close proximity to one another. The first is highly innovative and is constantly initiating new programs, creative services, and effective forms of public relations. The second imitates the first, neither requesting permission nor acknowledging the influence. Any ethical problem here?

11. Because of existing staff patterns and uneven annual work flow, catalog librarians are asked to type their own stencils for two weeks twice a year. Ought they to accede in this expectation or, by refusing, force a management restructuring which would rid them of this nonprofessional task?

12. Should a library build a circulation routine upon use of patrons' Social Security numbers for ID purposes, in view of the apprehension felt in some quarters that extensive use of Social Security numbers contains a threat of intrusion of individual privacy?

13. Ought researchers be permitted to submit phony questions to reference staff for purposes of library evaluation, without the staff's knowledge that it is being so tested?
14. Should a retired librarian volunteer to work in a library that is about to be closed for lack of funds?
15. Does a library have an ethical obligation to make an employee's personnel file available for his or her examination?
16. How can a librarian determine to what amount his research expenses (e.g., photocopying, stationery, etc.), or his expenses in performing a service for a professional association, can appropriately be charged to the library? Does the situation change if these incidental expenses are incurred in the performance of a paid consultancy?

Reference librarians face a variety of ethical dilemmas in the normal execution of their jobs. For years they have expressed concern about their personal liability for dissemination of legal or medical information. Personal ethics and professional ethical responsibility have to be separated intellectually and emotionally, especially if the constituency one serves has a set of mores which are strong. Some typical questions include: What are the personal and professional conflicts in providing information on contraceptives or abortion? Of what effect is the age of the patron? How do your personal religious beliefs or practices affect the tone or quality of the response? Does geography play a role?

John C. Swan applied the 1981 Code of Ethics to the practice and performance of reference librarians in "Ethics at the Reference Desk: Comfortable Theories and Tricky Practices."[3] Swan raised for all librarians the need to face some uncomfortable, yet provocative questions, citing Robert Hauptman's well-known "bomb experiment" where 13 librarians were approached with three questions: (1) Are you the reference librarian? (2) I need some information for the construction of a small explosive device. I am interested in the chemical properties of cordite— perhaps in a handbook? (3) What I want to know is the potency of this chemical—whether a small amount will blow up, say, a normal surburan house?[4] Hauptman charged the 13 librarians with unethical behavior, regardless of the grounds on which they chose to provide him with the information which he requested. Swan disagreed with Hauptman and pointed to the "pitfalls that await anyone who tries to impose moral simplicity upon ethical complexity."[5]

Basing ethics on morality can lead to the pitfalls to which Swan points. Basing morality on ethics, however, keeps one aware of the complexity of the judgments required for each of us to provide good library service as a librarian with a sense of personal and professional ethical satisfaction.

References

1. International City Managers Association, "Are You an Ethical Employee?" *Public Management* 64 (5) (May 1962): 20ff.
2. Donn B. Parker, *Ethical Conflict in Computer Science and Technology: Workbook* (Menlo Park, CA: SRI International), p. 50.
3. John C. Swan, "Ethics at the Reference Desk: Comfortable Theories and Tricky Practices," *The Reference Librarian* (New York: Haworth Press, 1982): pp. 99ff.
4. Robert Hauptman, "Professionalism or Culpability? An Experiment in Ethics," *Library Lit 7—The Best of 1976,* ed. Bill Katz (Metuchen, NJ: Scarecrow, 1977), p. 322; originally in *Wilson Library Bulletin* 50 (8) (April 1976): 626–27.
5. Swan, p. 113.

Selected Bibliography

Professional Ethics, General

American Society of Civil Engineers. *Conference on Engineering Ethics*. New York: The Society, 1975.

Association of American University Professors. "Statement on Professional Ethics." *New Directions for Higher Education* 9 (1) (1981): 83–85.

Asheim, Lester. "Librarians as Professionals." *Library Trends* 27 (3) (Winter 1979): 225–27.

Bayles, Michael D. *Professional Ethics*. Belmont, CA: Wadsworth Publishing Company, 1981.

Birdsall, William. "Librarianship, Professionalism, and Social Change." *Library Journal* 107 (3) (February 1, 1982): 223–26.

Bolton, Charles Knowles. "The Ethics of Librarianship—A Proposal for a Revised Code." *The Annals* of the American Academy of Political and Social Science 101 (May 1922): 138ff.

Bowman, James S. "Ethics and the Public Service: A Selected and Annotated Bibliography." *Public Personnel Management Journal* 10 (1) (Winter 1981): 179–99.

Broehl, Wayne G., Jr. "Insights into Business and Society." *Harvard Business Review* 44 (3) (May–June 1966): 6–15.

Calk, R.; Frankel, M. S.; and Chafer, S. B. *Professional Ethics Activities in the Scientific and Engineering Societies*. Washington, DC: AAAS, 1980.

Chandler, Ralph Clark. "The Problem of Moral Reasoning in American Public Administration: The Case for a Code of Ethics." *Public Administration Review* 43 (1) (January/February 1983): 32–39.

Churchill, Larry R. "The Teaching of Ethics and Moral Values in Teaching." *Journal of Higher Education,* Special Issue on Ethics and the Academic Profession 3 (3) (May–June 1982): 296–306.

"City Management Code of Ethics." *Public Management* 63 (3) (March 1981): 1–22.

"Code of Ethics for Personnel Administration." *Personnel Journal* 38 (2) (June 1959): 62–63.

"A Code of Ethics for Social Studies Professions." *Social Education* 45 (6) (October 1981): 451–53.

Cohn, Steven M. "The Ethical Thicket of Academic Autonomy." *The Chronicle of Higher Education* 25 (21) (February 2, 1983): 64.

"Computer Ethics: New Questions Arise over Misuse in American Business." *The New York Times* (December 25, 1983).

Crickman, Robin D. "The Emerging Information Professional." *Library Trends* 28 (2) (Fall 1979): 311–27.

Dobel, J. Patrick. "Doing Good by Staying In?" *Public Personnel Management Journal* 11 (2) (Spring 1982): 126–39.

Douglas, Paul H. *Ethics in Government*. Cambridge, MA: Harvard University Press, 1952.

Durkheim, Emil. *Professional Ethics and American Morals*. Glencoe, IL: The Free Press, 1958.

Durrance, Joan C. "The Generic Librarian: Anonymity versus Accountability." *RQ* 22 (3) (Spring 1983): 278–83.

Elliott, Phillip. *The Sociology of the Professions*. New York: Herder and Herder, 1972.

"Employer Gets Less Stress in Revised ALA Ethics Code." *Library Journal* 104 (22) (December 15, 1979).

Ennis, Philip H. "Seven Questions about the Profession of Librarianship: Introduction." *Library Quarterly* 31 (4) (October 1961): 299–400.

"Ethical Responsibilities of College Professors." Letters to the Editor, *Chronicle of Higher Education* 36 (3) (March 16, 1983).

"Ethics: Dictates and Dilemmas." *Public Management*, Special Issue on ICMA Code of Ethics 63 (3) (March 1981).

"Ethics in Personnel Administration." *Personnel* 30 (3) (November 1953): 180–86.

Fields, Cheryl M. "Nurses' Central Role in Sensitive Health-Care Dilemmas Leads to Renewed Emphasis on Professional Ethics." *The Chronicle of Higher Education* 37 (2) (September 7, 1983): 16.

Fleishman, Joel L., and Payne, Bruce L. *Ethical Dilemmas and the Education of Policy Makers*. Hastings-on-Hudson, NY: The Hastings Institute, 1980.

Fletcher, Joseph. *Situational Ethics: The New Morality*. Philadelphia, PA: Westminster Press, 1966.

Foster, Gregory D. "Law Morality, and the Public Servant." *Public Administration Review* 41 (1) (January–February 1981): 29–33.

Freedman, Monroe H. ". . . Wrong? Silence Is Right." *New York Times* (February 14, 1983).

Fromm, Erich. *Man for Himself: An Inquiry into the Psychology of Ethics*. New York: Fawcett, 1978.

Ganett, Thomas M. *Ethics in Business*. New York: Sheed and Ward, 1963.

Gillers, Stephen. "Lawyers' Silence: Wrong. . ." *New York Times* (February 14, 1983).

Goode, William J. "The Librarian: From Occupation to Profession?" *Library Quarterly* 31 (4) (October 1961): 306–20.

Gordis, Robert. *Politics and Ethics*. Santa Barbara, CA: Center for the Study of Democratic Institutions, 1961.

Greenfield, Meg. "Politics, Scandals, and Ethics." *Newsweek* (July 11, 1983): 80.

Hampshire, Stuart, ed. *Public and Private Morality*. Cambridge, England: Cambridge University Press, 1978.

Hartwig, Richard. "Ethics and Organizational Structure." *The Bureaucrat* 9 (4) (Winter 1981): 48–56.

Hauptman, Robert. "Ethical Commitment and the Professions." *Catholic Library World* 51 (5) (December 1979): 196–99.

———. "Professionalism or Culpability? An Experiment in Ethics." *Wilson Library Bulletin* 50 (8) (April 1976): 626–27.

Heller, Harold, and Ridehour, Nancy. "Professional Standards: Foundation for the Future." *Exceptional Children* 49 (4) (January 1983): 294–98.

Hill, Thomas E. *Ethics in Theory and Practice*. New York: Thomas Y. Crowell Co., 1956.

Hochbaum, Godfrey M. "Ethical Dilemmas in Health Education." *Health Education* 11 (2) (March/April 1980): 4–9.

Howe, Elizabeth, and Kaufman, J. "The Ethics of Contemporary American Planners." *The APA Journal* 45 (3) (July 1979): 243–54.

Kattsoff, Louis O. *Making Moral Decisions, an Existential Analysis*. The Hague, Netherlands: Martinies Nijhoff, 1965.

Katz, Bill, and Fraley, Ruth, eds. *Ethics and Reference Service*. New York: Haworth Press, 1982.

Kellogg, Marion S. "The Ethics of Employee Appraisal." *Personnel* 42 (4) (July–August 1965).

Kernaghan, Kenneth. "Codes of Ethics and Public Administration: Progress, Problems and Prospects." *Public Administration* (59) (Summer 1980): 207–23.

Kolata, Ging. "Caltech Torn by Dispute over Software." *Science* 220 (4600) (May 27, 1983): 932–34.

Laeusch, Carl F. *Professional and Business Ethics*. New York: Henry Holt and Co., 1926.

Leip, Wayne A. *Ethics for Policy Decisions: The Art of Asking Deliberative Questions*. Englewood Cliffs, NJ: Prentice-Hall, 1952.

Lynn, Kenneth, and the Editors of *Daedalus*. *The Professions in America*. Boston: Houghton Mifflin, 1965.

McCoy, Bowen H. "The Parable of the Sadhu." *Harvard Business Review* 61 (5) (September–October 1983): 103–08.

MacIntyre, Alasdair. *A Short History of Ethics*. New York: Macmillan, 1973.

Mertins, Herman, Jr., and Henigan, Patrick J., eds. *Applying Professional Standards and Ethics in the Eighties/A Workbook and Study Guide for Public Administrators*. Washington, DC: American Society for Public Administration, 1982.

Miles, Rufus E., Jr. *Awakening from the American Dream: The Loud and Political Limits to Growth*. New York: Universe Books, 1976.

Orkin, Mark M. *Legal Ethics and Professional Conduct*. Toronto, ON: Cartwright and Sons, 1957.

Parker, Donn B. *Ethical Conflicts in Computer Science and Technology*. Arlington, VA: AFIPS Press, n.d.

Peters, Harold H. *Ethics for Today*. New York: American Book Company, 1957.

Peterson, Kenneth G. "Ethics in Academic Librarianship: The Need for Values." *The Journal of Academic Librarianship* 9 (3) (July 1983): 132–37.

Prentice, Ann, and Arden, Caroline. "Can Ethics Provide the Answers?" *Footnotes (ALA/JMRT)* 13 (1) (September 1983).

Reynolds, Charles H. "Developing the New Field of Bioveterinary Ethics." Paper presented at ethics seminar, University of Tennessee, Spring 1983.

Rohr, John A. "The Problem of Professional Ethics." *The Bureaucrat* 11 (2) (Summer 1982): 47–50.

Ross, W. D. *The Right and the Good*. Oxford, England: Clarendon Press, 1930.

Schiller, Anita. "Who Can Own What American Knows?" *Nation* (April 17, 1982): 461–63.

Schmidt, Warren H., and Posner, Barry Z. *Managerial Values in Perspective*. New York: American Management Association, 1983.

Schur, George M. "Toward a Code of Ethics for Academics." *Journal of Higher Education* 3 (3) (May/June 1982): 318–34.

Sjoherg, Gideon. *Ethics, Politics and Social Research*. Cambridge, MA: Schenkman Publishing Company, 1971.

Slowik, Stanley M. "The Manager as Moralist." *Management World* 10 (10) (October 1981): 25–27.

Taylor, Stuart, Jr. "ABA's Decision: Lawyer Confidentiality over Disclosure of Crimes-to-Be." *New York Times* (February 14, 1983).

————. "Ethics Code Isn't Open and Shut." *New York Times* (August 7, 1983).

Titus, Harold H. *Ethics for Today*. Boston: American Book Company, 1936.

Tuma, Nancy Brandon, and Grimes, Andrew J. "A Comparison of Models of Role Orientations of Professionals in a Research-Oriented University." *Administrative Science Quarterly* 26 (2) (1981): 187–206.

Twedt, Dick Warren. "Why a Marketing Research Code of Ethics?" *Journal of Marketing* 27 (4) (October 6, 1963): 48–50.

U.S. General Accounting Office. "Framework for Assessing Job Vulnerability to Ethical Problems." Study by the Staff of the U.S. General Accounting Office. Washington, DC: GAO, 1981.

Vollmer, Howard M., and Mills, Donald T., eds. *Professionalization*. Englewood Cliffs, NJ: Prentice-Hall, 1966.

Wachs, Martin. "Ethical Dilemmas in Forecasting for Public Policy." *Public Administration Review* 42 (6) (November/December 1982): 562–67.

Walker, Donald E. "The President as Ethical Leader of the Campus." *New Directions for Higher Education* 9 (1) (1981): 15–27.

Ward, Leo R. *Ethics and the Social Sciences*. Notre Dame, IN: University of Notre Dame Press, 1955.

Werner, Simcha B. "New Directions in the Study of Administrative Corruption." *Public Administration Review* 43 (2) (March/April 1983): 146–54.

Winter, Gibson. *Elements for a Social Ethics: Scientific and Ethical Perspectives on Social Process.* New York: Macmillan, 1966.

Wylie, Irving. *The Self-Made Man in America.* New Brunswick, NJ: Rutgers University Press, 1954.

Professional Ethics, Library Literature*

American Library Association. Association for Library Service to Children. "ALSC Policy for Membership on Award and Media Evaluation Committees." *Top of the News* 38 (Spring 1982): 184–85.

American Library Association. Florida Association for Media in Education. "FAME Code of Ethics for Education Media Professionals (Preliminary Draft)." *Florida Media Quarterly* 5 (Winter 1980): 15–17.

American Library Association. Professional Ethics Committee. "On Professional Ethics (Final Draft of Revised Statement and Code)." *American Libraries* 12 (June 1981): 335.

American Library Association. Professional Ethics Committee. "Statement of Professional Ethics (Final Draft of Revised Statement)." *Arkansas Libraries* 38 (June 1981): 27.

American Library Association. Professional Ethics Committee. "Statement on Professional Ethics (1979 Draft)." *School Library Journal* 26 (November 1979): 14; *American Libraries* 10 (December 1979): 666; *Wilson Library Bulletin* 54 (December 1979): 217.

American Library Association. Society of American Archivists. "Code of Ethics for Archivists." *American Archivist* 43 (Summer 1980): 414–18.

American Library Association. Special Committee on Code of Ethics. "Statement of Professional Ethics (1975)." *School Library Journal* 26 (November 1979): 14; *American Libraries* 10 (December 1979): 666.

---

*Library Literature, 1955–1983, search under the following headings: Education for Librarianship, Ethics, Librarianship—Aims & Objectives, Librarianship—Philosophical Aspects, Librarianship—Social Aspects, Librarianship as a Profession, Library Schools—Curricula, Library Science—Teaching, Professional Ethics (see Ethics).

American Library Association. Special Committee on Code of Ethics. "Statement on Professional Ethics, 1975." *American Libraries* 6 (April 1975): 231.

Anderson, LeMoyne W., and Kell, Bea L. "Human Relations Training for Librarians?" *College & Research Libraries* 19 (May 1958): 227–29.

Asheim, Lester E. "Training Needs of Librarians Doing Adult Education Work: A Report of the Allerton Park Conference." *American Library Association Journal* (November 14–16, 1954): 1955.

"Aslib and Ethics (Opposing the Application of the Draft Code of Librarians Outside the Public Area)." *Library Association Record* 83 (June 1981): 278.

Bandix, Dorothy. "Teaching the Concept of Intellectual Freedom: The State of the Art." *American Library Association Bulletin* 63 (March 1969): 351–62.

Bearman, Toni Carbo. "Do We Need a Code of Ethics for Information Science?" *ASIS Bulletin* 8 (October 1981): 36.

Berninghausen, David Knipe. "Teaching a Commitment to Intellectual Freedom." *Library Journal* 92 (December 15, 1967): 3601–05.

Berry, John Nichols, III. "Sharing the Bad News." *Library Journal* 101 (June 1, 1976): 1239.

Borchardt, D. H. "Prolegomena to an Australian Code of Professional Ethics for Librarians." *Australian Academic and Research Libraries* 12 (December 1981): 248–59.

Brees, M. A. "Challenge for Library Schools: A Student's View." *Special Libraries* 64 (October 1973): 433–38.

Canadian Library Association. "Code of Ethics." *UNABASHED Librarian* 34 (1980): 31.

Carnovsky, Leon. "Changing Patterns in Librarianship: Implications for Library Education." *Wilson Library Bulletin* 431 (January 1967): 484–91.

———. "Library in Society." The Orientation Course at the Graduate Library School of the University of Chicago. In *Association of American Library Schools* (meeting minutes, 1956, Miami Beach) pp. 6–13.

Carroll, Carmal Edward. "Professionalization of Education for Librarianship with Special Reference to the Years 1940–1960." Metuchen, NJ: Scarecrow Press, 1971, p. 355.

Crawford, Helen. "In Search of an Ethic of Medical Librarianship." *Medical Library Association Bulletin* 66 (July 1978): 331–37.

Dain, Phyllis. "Profession and the Professors." *Library Journal* 105 (February 1, 1981): 1701–07; discussion 106 (February 1, 1981): 279.

"Employer Gets Less Stress in Revised ALA Ethics Code." *Library Journal* 104 (December 15, 1979): 2609.

Fitzgibbons, Shirley A. "Professionalism and Ethical Behavior: Relationship to School Library Media Personnel." *School Media Quarterly* 8 (Winter 1980): 82–100+.

Flanagan, Leo Nelson. "Comment by L. N. Flanagan." *Wilson Library Bulletin* 54 (May 1980): 550.

"Florida Association for Media Education Media Professionals." *Florida Media Quarterly* 6 (Summer 1981): 22–23.

Gibson, Mary C. "Preparing Librarians to Serve Handicapped Individuals." *Journal of Education for Librarianship* 18 (Fall 1977): 121–30.

Goode, William J. "Librarian: From Occupation to Profession?" *Library Quarterly* 31 (October 1961): 306–20.

Greenwood, T. "Professional Ethics." *New Library World* 82 (July 1981): 123–24.

Harlow, Neal R. "Character and Responsibility of a Graduate School; With Comments by a Number of Distinguished Library Educators." *Library Journal* 93 (May 1, 1968): 1869–75.

Harvard-Williams, P. "Professional Education: A Personal View." *International Library Review* 13 (October 1981): 351–56.

Hauptman, Robert. "Ethical Commitment and the Professions." *Catholic Library World* 51 (December 1979): 196–99.

———. "Professionalism or Culpability? An Experiment in Ethics." *Wilson Library Bulletin* 50 (April 1976): 626–27.

Holley, Edward G. "Library Education and the Library Profession; Some Thoughts on What We Do, How Well We Do It, and Where We Go from Here." *Texas Library Journal* 53 (Spring 1977): 72–80.

———. "Renewing Our Faith in the Profession of Librarianship: Our Commitment to Serve." *Alabama Librarian* 25 (Spring 1974): 13–21.

Horrocks, Norman. "Library Education Issues in the U.S., Britain, and Canada." *Bowker Annual of Library and Book Trade Information.* 20th ed. New York: R. R. Bowker, 1975, pp. 323–28.

"Intellectual Freedom and Censorship Is the Title of a New Course at the Graduate School of Library Science at Simmons College." *Wilson Library Bulletin* 42 (January 1968): 454.

Kister, Kenneth F. "Education Librarians in Educational Freedom." *Library Trends* 19 (July 1970): 159–68.

Kister, Kenneth F., and Moone, E. E., eds. "Unique Course on Intellectual Freedom and Censorship." New York: R. R. Bowker, 1969, pp. 395–415.

Koehler, Boyd, and Coleman, J. "Professionalism: The Heart of the Matter." *Catholic Library World* 51 (February 1980): 291–95.

"LA Code of Ethics." *New Library World* 81 (December 1981): 235–36.

LaPorte, Margaret. "Confidentiality of Librarian/Patron Exchanges." *Connecticut Libraries* 23 (Spring 1981): 22–23.

"Library Code of Ethics." *Ohio Library Association* 36 (January 1976): 7–9.

Luckenbill, W. Bernard. "Teaching Helping Relationships, Concepts in the Reference Process." *Journal of Education Librarianship* 18 (Fall 1980): 110–20.

Marchant, Maurice P., and Lebare, L. "Library School Instruction in Discrimination Awareness." *American Libraries* 10 (January 1979): 42–43.

Melinat, Carl H. "Library in Society at Syracuse University." In *Association of American Library Schools* (meeting minutes, 1956, Miami Beach) pp. 14–18.

Monroe, Mabel Ester. "Educating Librarians for the Work of Library Adult Education." *Library Trends* 8 (July 1959): 91–107.

———. "Education in Librarianship for Serving the Disadvantaged." *Library Trends* 20 (October 1971): 445–62.

———. "Toward Library Social Action." *Wisconsin Library Bulletin* 69 (March 1973): 92–94.

Moon, Eric. "Ethical Bones." *Library Journal* 93 (January 15, 1968): 131.

Nelson, Milo Gabriel. "Starting Out in the Eighties (Adjust to New Ways of Thinking about Librarianship)." *Wilson Library Bulletin* 56 (October 1981): 85.

"Our Ethical Duty in a Free, Civilized Society (Draft Code for Professional Ethics)." *Library Association Record* 83 (August 1981): 367.

Peterson, Kenneth G. "Ethics in Academic Librarianship: The Need for Values." *The Journal of Academic Librarianship* 9 (July 1983): 132–37.

Ratner, J. F. "Library Professional: An Alternative View." *Michigan Librarian* 45 (Winter 1979): 7.

Reed, Sarah Rebecca. "Trends in Professional Education." *Drexel Library Quarterly* 3 (January 1967): 1–24.

Reid, Marion T. "Off the Cuff Advice for the 'Green' MLS (or Anyone Else Starting a New Job)." *Louisiana Library Association Bulletin* 38 (Spring 1975): 3–5.

"St. John's University Is Offering a Drug Information Specialist Program." *Catholic Library World* 50 (September 1978): 87.

Sargent, Charles William. "Individual Conscience (Science Looks to the Future in Terms of Quality Information Services)." *ASIS Bulletin* 5 (October 1978): 36.

Shaw, Ralph R. "Library's Role in Society Today?" *Journal of Education for Librarianship* 2 (Spring 1962): 177–82.

Shores, Louis. "Prologue to a National Plan: The Professional Association's Responsibility toward Education in Library Science Bibliography." *Southwestern Librarian* 13 (Summer 1963): 88–96.

Shuman, Bruce A. "Intellectual Freedom Courses in Graduate Library Schools." *Journal of Education for Librarianship* 18 (Fall 1977): 99–109.

"Simmons Announces Course on Intellectual Freedom." *Library Journal* 94 (22) (December 15, 1969): 4455.

"Some Thoughts on What Makes a 'Professional Librarian' by a Writer Who Preferred to Remain Nameless." *Wyoming Library Roundup* 34 (December 1978): 9.

Trejo, Arnulfo Duenes. "Modifying Library Education for Ethnic Imperatives." *American Libraries* 8 (March 1977): 150–51.

"USC Censorship Courses to Break New Ground." *Library Journal* 94 (November 1969): 3948.

Usherwood, R. C. "Towards a Code of Professional Ethics." *Aslib Proceedings* 33 (June 1981): 233–43.

————. "Feeling the Draft: Quality in our (LA) Ethical Debate." *Library Association Record* 83 (May 1981): 246–47.

Wasserman, Paul. *New Librarianship: A Challenge for Change*. New York: R. R. Bowker, 1972.

"What Is a Profession?" *New Library World* 83 (October 1981): 179–98.

Willard, Derald Dean. "Three Areas of Need for Training in Librarianship in Indiana." *Library Occurrent* 24 (November 1974): 495–500.

Index